home baked

MUFFINS PASTRIES CAKES BISCUITS

home baked

MUFFINS PASTRIES CAKES BISCUITS

THE AUSTRALIAN
Women's Weekly

Contents

Baker's delight

I love baking. Of all the kitchen arts, it's baking that has sustained my interest and enthusiasm for cooking all these years. It impacts on all my senses: I feel dough becoming warm and alive in my hands as I knead it; I hear the song a perfectly baked butter cake sings when it's taken from the oven; I adore the way my house smells in winter when the aroma of baking bread wafts down the hallway; I'm still amazed that the combination of a few simple dry and wet ingredients can be visually transformed into something truly "pretty as a picture"; and I'm more than happy when a cake tastes "right" as well as delicious. So it's with great pleasure that I introduce you to this wonderful book – hoping that it helps reassure you that baking is neither difficult nor time-consuming, and that it whets your creative appetite for baking at home for friends and family.

Pamela Clark
FOOD DIRECTOR

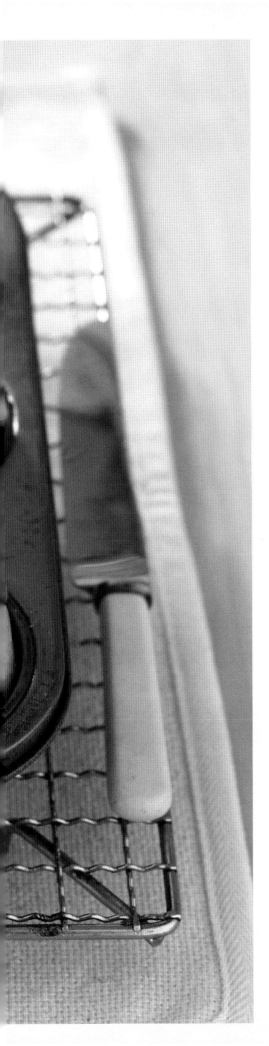

Muffins

marvellous muffins

Muffins are simple to make and delicious eaten hot, warm or cold, with or without butter.

MIXING

It is important not to overmix the muffin mixture; it requires minimum mixing and should look coarse and lumpy.

PAN SIZES

We used a medium-sized muffin pan (⅓-cup/80ml capacity), and a larger, texas-style muffin pan (¾ cup/180ml capacity). Other sized pans are available, but you will need to adjust cooking times if you use these pans. Pans should be slightly more than half-filled with mixture, whatever size you use. Pans should be greased evenly or coated with non-stick spray.

TESTING WHEN COOKED

Muffins are cooked when they are browned, risen, firm to touch and beginning to shrink from the sides of the pan. If in doubt, push a metal or wooden skewer into a muffin. When withdrawn, the skewer should be clean and free from muffin mixture.

STORING

Muffins are at their best made on the day of serving; however, they can be stored in an airtight container for up to two days. Muffins can be frozen, either individually wrapped in foil or together in a sealed container, for up to three months.

To thaw frozen muffins, either place muffins, covered in foil, on an oven tray, or wrap individual muffins in foil; thaw in moderate oven about 20 minutes. Individual unwrapped muffins can be thawed in a microwave oven on HIGH (100%) for about 30 seconds.

For an appealing look, line muffin pans with pretty paper cases.

Various sized pans can be used, but cooking times need to be adjusted.

Do not overmix the muffin mixture, it should look coarse and lumpy.

Fill muffin holes or paper cases as instructed in recipe.

PREPARATION TIME 10 MINUTES
COOKING TIME 35 MINUTES

2¼ cups (335g) self-raising flour

1 cup (220g) caster sugar

1 teaspoon vanilla extract

2 eggs, beaten lightly

100g butter, melted

1 cup (250ml) milk

1 teaspoon grated lemon rind

200g fresh or frozen mixed berries

mixed berry muffins

1 Preheat oven to moderately hot. Grease six-hole (¾-cup/180ml) texas muffin pan or spray six large disposable muffin cases and place on an oven tray.

2 Sift flour into large bowl; add sugar then combined extract, egg, butter, milk and rind. Add berries; stir through gently.

3 Divide muffin mixture among holes of prepared pans.

4 Bake muffins in moderately hot oven about 35 minutes. Stand muffins in pan for a few minutes before turning onto wire rack.

makes 6

Taste-test combinations when berries are
in season and freeze your favourites.

raspberry and coconut muffins

PREPARATION TIME 10 MINUTES
COOKING TIME 20 MINUTES

1 Preheat oven to moderately hot. Grease 12-hole (⅓-cup/80ml) muffin pan.

2 Place flour in large bowl; using fingertips, rub in butter. Add sugar, buttermilk, egg, desiccated coconut and raspberries; mix until just combined.

3 Divide mixture among holes of prepared pan; sprinkle with shredded coconut.

4 Bake muffins in moderately hot oven about 20 minutes. Stand muffins in pan for a few minutes before turning onto wire rack.

makes 12

2½ cups (375g) self-raising flour

90g butter, chopped

1 cup (220g) caster sugar

1¼ cups (310ml) buttermilk

1 egg, beaten lightly

⅓ cup (30g) desiccated coconut

150g fresh or frozen raspberries

2 tablespoons shredded coconut

Two kinds of coconut – finely grated in the mix and shredded on top – create a moist morsel with a contrasting crunch.

PREPARATION TIME 15 MINUTES
COOKING TIME 25 MINUTES

2 cups (300g) self-raising flour

⅓ cup (50g) plain flour

½ teaspoon bicarbonate of soda

½ cup (110g) firmly packed brown sugar

¼ cup (60ml) maple-flavoured syrup

⅔ cup mashed banana

2 eggs, beaten lightly

1 cup (250ml) buttermilk

⅓ cup (80ml) vegetable oil

COCONUT TOPPING

15g butter

1 tablespoon maple-flavoured syrup

⅔ cup (30g) flaked coconut

banana maple muffins

You will need about two small (260g) over-ripe bananas for this recipe.

1 Preheat oven to moderately hot. Grease 12-hole (⅓-cup/80ml) muffin pan.

2 Make coconut topping.

3 Sift dry ingredients into large bowl. Stir in maple syrup and banana, then egg, buttermilk and oil.

4 Divide mixture among holes of prepared pan; sprinkle with coconut topping.

5 Bake muffins in moderately hot oven about 20 minutes. Stand muffins in pan for a few minutes before turning onto wire rack.

COCONUT TOPPING Melt butter in small saucepan, add maple syrup and coconut; stir constantly over high heat until coconut is browned lightly. Remove from heat.

makes 12

Serve with crispy bacon for a scrumptious brunch with a difference.

ginger date muffins with caramel sauce

PREPARATION TIME 15 MINUTES
COOKING TIME 35 MINUTES

1 Preheat oven to moderately hot. Grease 12-hole (⅓-cup/80ml) muffin pan.

2 Combine dates and water in small saucepan, bring to a boil; remove from heat, add soda, stand 5 minutes.

3 Meanwhile, sift dry ingredients into large bowl, stir in date mixture and remaining ingredients.

4 Divide mixture among holes of prepared pan.

5 Bake muffins in moderately hot oven about 20 minutes. Stand muffins in pan for a few minutes before turning onto wire rack. Serve warm muffins drizzled with caramel sauce.

CARAMEL SAUCE Combine ingredients in medium saucepan. Stir over heat, without boiling, until sugar is dissolved, then simmer, without stirring, about 3 minutes or until thickened slightly.

makes 12

1 cup (160g) seeded chopped dates

⅓ cup (80ml) water

¼ teaspoon bicarbonate of soda

2 cups (300g) self-raising flour

1 cup (150g) plain flour

2 teaspoons ground ginger

½ teaspoon mixed spice

1 cup (220g) firmly packed brown sugar

2 teaspoons grated orange rind

1 egg, beaten lightly

1¼ cups (310ml) milk

¼ cup (60ml) vegetable oil

CARAMEL SAUCE

1 cup (220g) firmly packed brown sugar

1 cup (250ml) cream

40g butter

Fresh cream or a dollop of ice-cream makes this a delicious dessert.

PREPARATION TIME 15 MINUTES

COOKING TIME 20 MINUTES

marmalade almond muffins

2 cups (300g) self-raising flour

125g butter, chopped

1 cup (80g) flaked almonds

⅔ cup (150g) caster sugar

1 tablespoon finely grated orange rind

½ cup (170g) orange marmalade

2 eggs, beaten lightly

½ cup (125ml) milk

¼ cup (20g) flaked almonds, extra

ORANGE SYRUP

¼ cup (85g) orange marmalade

2 tablespoons water

1 Preheat oven to moderately hot. Grease 12-hole (⅓-cup/80ml) muffin pan.

2 Sift flour into large bowl, rub in butter. Stir in nuts, sugar and rind, then marmalade, egg and milk.

3 Divide mixture among holes of prepared pan; sprinkle with extra nuts.

4 Bake muffins in moderately hot oven about 20 minutes. Stand muffins in pan for a few minutes before turning onto wire rack.

5 Meanwhile, combine orange syrup ingredients in small bowl. Drizzle syrup over warm muffins.

makes 12

Serve warm for a perfect afternoon tea.

citrus poppy seed muffins

PREPARATION TIME 15 MINUTES
COOKING TIME 20 MINUTES

1 Preheat oven to moderately hot. Grease 12-hole (⅓-cup/80ml) muffin pan.

2 Combine butter, rinds, caster sugar, egg, sifted flour and milk in medium bowl; beat with electric mixer until just combined. Increase speed to medium; beat until mixture is just changed in colour; stir in poppy seeds.

3 Divide mixture among holes of prepared pan.

4 Bake muffins in moderately hot oven about 20 minutes. Stand muffins in pan for a few minutes before turning onto wire rack.

5 Peel rind thinly from orange, avoiding any white pith. Cut rind into thin strips. To serve, dust muffins with icing sugar mixture; top with orange strips.

makes 12

125g softened butter, chopped

2 teaspoons finely grated lemon rind

2 teaspoons finely grated lime rind

2 teaspoons finely grated orange rind

⅔ cup (150g) caster sugar

2 eggs, beaten lightly

2 cups (300g) self-raising flour

½ cup (250ml) milk

2 tablespoons poppy seeds

1 medium orange (240g)

icing sugar mixture, for dusting

Tiny, blue-grey poppy seeds add texture and a slightly nutty taste.

apple and custard muffins

PREPARATION TIME 20 MINUTES
COOKING TIME 25 MINUTES

90g butter, melted

2 cups (300g) self-raising flour

1 cup (150g) plain flour

½ teaspoon ground cinnamon

¾ cup (165g) caster sugar

1 egg, beaten lightly

1 cup (250ml) milk

¼ cup (60ml) packaged thick custard

½ cup (110g) canned pie apples

2 tablespoons brown sugar

½ teaspoon ground cinnamon, extra

1 Preheat oven to moderately hot. Grease 12-hole (⅓-cup/80ml) muffin pan, or line with paper patty cases.

2 Combine butter, flours, cinnamon, caster sugar, egg and milk in large bowl; stir until just combined.

3 Divide half the mixture among holes of prepared pan; make well in centre of each muffin, drop 1 level teaspoon of custard and 2 level teaspoons of apple into each well. Top with remaining muffin mixture; sprinkle with combined brown sugar and extra cinnamon.

4 Bake muffins in moderately hot oven about 25 minutes. Stand muffins in pan for a few minutes before turning onto wire rack.

makes 12

A crumbly topping hides a surprise.

honey sultana
and pecan muffins

PREPARATION TIME 10 MINUTES
COOKING TIME 25 MINUTES

You will need about two small (260g) over-ripe bananas
for this recipe.

1 Preheat oven to moderately hot. Grease 12-hole (⅓-cup/80ml) muffin pan.

2 Sift flour and cinnamon into large bowl. Add sugar, nuts and sultanas, then combined remaining ingredients. Stir until ingredients just combined.

3 Divide mixture among holes of prepared pan.

4 Bake muffins in moderately hot oven about 25 minutes. Stand muffins in pan for a few minutes before turning onto wire rack. Dust with sifted icing sugar and top with a light sprinkling of cinnamon, if desired.

makes 12

2 cups (300g) self-raising flour

2 teaspoons ground cinnamon

¾ cup (150g) firmly packed brown sugar

½ cup (50g) chopped pecans

½ cup (80g) sultanas

¼ cup (90g) honey

⅔ cup mashed banana

¼ cup (70g) low-fat yoghurt

¾ cup (180ml) low-fat milk

2 eggs, beaten lightly

Low in fat, big on flavour, these moist muffins
are perfect for a picnic.

PREPARATION TIME 10 MINUTES (PLUS
REFRIGERATION TIME)
COOKING TIME 20 MINUTES

overnight date
and muesli muffins

1¼ cups (185g) plain flour

1¼ cups (160g) toasted muesli

1 teaspoon ground cinnamon

1 teaspoon bicarbonate of soda

½ cup (110g) firmly packed brown sugar

½ cup (30g) unprocessed bran

¾ cup (120g) coarsely chopped
seedless dates

1½ cups (375ml) buttermilk

½ cup (125ml) vegetable oil

1 egg, beaten lightly

1 Combine ingredients in large bowl, stir until just combined. Cover, refrigerate overnight.

2 Preheat oven to moderately hot. Grease 12-hole (⅓-cup/80ml) muffin pan.

3 Divide mixture among holes of prepared pan.

4 Bake muffins in moderately hot oven about 20 minutes. Stand muffins in pan for a few minutes before turning onto wire rack.

makes 12

A filling, classic, healthy muffin that is simple to prepare.

choc brownie muffins

PREPARATION TIME 15 MINUTES
COOKING TIME 20 MINUTES

1 Preheat oven to moderately hot. Grease 12-hole (⅓-cup/80ml) muffin pan.

2 Sift dry ingredients into large bowl; stir in remaining ingredients.

3 Divide mixture among holes of prepared pan.

4 Bake muffins in moderately hot oven about 20 minutes. Stand muffins in pan for a few minutes before turning onto wire rack. Dust with sifted extra cocoa, if desired.

makes 12

2 cups (300g) self-raising flour

⅓ cup (35g) cocoa powder

⅓ cup (75g) caster sugar

60g butter, melted

½ cup (95g) Choc Bits

½ cup (75g) pistachios, chopped coarsely

½ cup (165g) Nutella

1 egg, beaten lightly

¾ cup (180ml) milk

½ cup (120g) sour cream

Take care not to overcook these little indulgences – they should be slightly moist in the middle.

white chocolate and macadamia muffins

PREPARATION TIME 10 MINUTES
COOKING TIME 20 MINUTES

2 cups (300g) self-raising flour

⅔ cup (150g) caster sugar

¾ cup (140g) white Choc Bits

½ cup (75g) coarsely chopped macadamias, toasted

60g butter, melted

¾ cup (180ml) milk

1 egg, beaten lightly

1 Preheat oven to moderately hot. Grease six-hole (¾-cup/180ml) texas muffin pan.

2 Sift flour and sugar into large bowl; stir in remaining ingredients. Divide mixture among holes of prepared pan.

3 Bake muffins in moderately hot oven about 20 minutes. Stand muffins in pan for a few minutes before turning onto wire rack.

makes 6

Play with a theme of white on white – plates, serviettes and mugs of hot white chocolate.

gluten-free, dairy-free raspberry muffins

PREPARATION TIME 15 MINUTES
COOKING TIME 20 MINUTES

1 Preheat oven to moderately hot. Grease 12-hole (⅓-cup/80ml) muffin pan, or line with paper patty cases.

2 Sift flour, baking powder and soda into large bowl. Stir in bran, sugar, combined milk, extract, spread and egg until almost combined. Add raspberries, stir until just combined.

3 Divide mixture among muffin holes; sprinkle with coffee crystals.

4 Bake in moderately hot oven about 20 minutes. Stand muffins in pan for a few minutes before carefully removing from pan to cool on wire rack.

makes 12

2½ cups (375g) gluten-free plain flour

1 tablespoon gluten-free baking powder

½ teaspoon bicarbonate of soda

⅓ cup (40g) rice bran

⅔ cup (150g) firmly packed brown sugar

1½ cups (375ml) soy milk

1 teaspoon vanilla extract

60g dairy-free spread, melted

2 eggs, beaten lightly

150g frozen raspberries

1 tablespoon coffee crystals

Fabulous for family or friends with allergies, a delight for everyone else.

Scones

Scones served hot from the oven with butter or jam and cream are delightful for morning or afternoon tea. There's no mystery to making light, fluffy scones; just follow our instructions.

basic scones

PREPARATION TIME 20 MINUTES
COOKING TIME 25 MINUTES

2½ cups (375g) self-raising flour

1 tablespoon caster sugar

¼ teaspoon salt

30g butter

¾ cup (180ml) milk

½ cup (125ml) water, approximately

1 Preheat oven to very hot. Grease deep 19cm-square cake pan.

2 Sift flour, sugar and salt into large bowl; rub in butter with fingertips.

3 Make well in centre of flour mixture; add milk and almost all of the water. Using a knife, "cut" the milk and water through the flour mixture to mix to a soft, sticky dough. Add remaining water only if needed for correct consistency.

4 Turn dough onto lightly floured surface; knead quickly and lightly until smooth.

5 Use hand to press dough out evenly to 2cm thickness.

6 Dip 4.5cm cutter into flour; cut as many rounds as you can from the piece of dough. Place scones side by side, just touching, in prepared pan. Gently knead scraps of dough together, and repeat pressing and cutting out of dough. Place rounds in prepared pan; brush tops with a little extra milk.

7 Bake scones in very hot oven about 15 minutes.

makes 16

MAKE A SOFT, STICKY DOUGH Most recipes give an approximate amount of liquid. The dough must be soft and sticky and just hold its shape when turned out.

USE MINIMUM FLOUR WHEN HANDLING DOUGH Turn dough onto lightly floured surface, dust your hands with flour and shape the dough into a ball by working the dough gently into a manageable, smooth shape. This will give you smooth-topped scones. Avoid excess flour, which upsets the balance of ingredients and interferes with the browning. Flatten the dough gently with your hand until it is an even thickness all over, press from the centre outwards. Use a floured, sharp metal cutter to cut scones from the dough; these scones will be the lightest. Lightly knead the scraps together. Press dough out again, slightly thicker to help make up for the second handling.

GLAZING We used a brush dipped in water, milk or egg. Water results in a light brown colour, egg in a golden brown colour and milk is a good compromise.

BAKE AT HIGH TEMPERATURES The oven temperature should be hot to very hot. The scones need to rise quickly to be light. We prefer to cook scones close together in lightly greased, shallow aluminium cake pans. This method gives the scones a "wall" to stop them toppling over, and allows them to brown evenly on top. They need to be cooked slightly longer than scones on oven trays. Don't squash scones into pan; they should be just touching (overcrowding makes it difficult to cook the scones in the middle of the pan).

TO TEST SCONES ARE COOKED Scones should be browned and sound hollow when tapped firmly on the top with your fingers. The scones in the middle are the ones to tap; they will take the longest to cook.

COOLING SCONES Always turn scones onto wire racks. If you prefer crusty scones, cool the scones uncovered. To soften the crust, wrap hot scones in a clean tea-towel.

scones

variations

1   SULTANA AND LEMON

When making the basic scone mixture, add ½ cup sultanas and 2 teaspoons grated lemon rind to flour mixture after the butter has been rubbed in.

2   CARDAMOM MARMALADE

When making the basic scone mixture, add 1 teaspoon ground cardamom and 2 teaspoons grated orange rind to flour mixture after the butter has been rubbed in. Also, omit the water and increase milk to 1 cup. Stir in ⅓ cup orange marmalade when adding milk.

3   BLUEBERRY GINGER

When making the basic scone mixture, add 3 teaspoons ground ginger and ½ cup fresh or frozen blueberries to flour mixture after the butter has been rubbed in.

4   BUTTERMILK

Replace the milk and the water in the basic scone mixture with approximately 1¼ cups buttermilk.

5   HONEY AND MUESLI

When making the basic scone mixture, add 1 teaspoon ground cinnamon and ½ cup toasted muesli to flour mixture after the butter has been rubbed in. Also, omit the water and add ¼ cup honey just before adding the milk.

6   APRICOT AND ALMOND

When making the basic scone mixture, add 1 teaspoon mixed spice, 1 cup chopped dried apricots and ⅓ cup chopped toasted slivered almonds to flour mixture after butter has been rubbed in.

1

2

3

4

5

6

Pastries

perfect pastry

KNEADING

Kneading really means turning the outside edges of a dough into the centre. When applied to most pastries it is not strictly kneading, just lightly working the dough into a manageable shape.

DO NOT OVER-HANDLE PASTRY

When kneading and rolling pastry, handle quickly, lightly and as little as possible. Heavy handling develops the gluten (protein) in the flour and toughens the pastry. Also, if the butter gets too soft it will be absorbed by the flour, resulting in a crust that is heavy and tough. Avoid re-rolling pastry scraps more than twice; pastry toughens each time it is rolled.

RESTING

Always "rest" pastry, wrapped in plastic, in the refrigerator for up to 30 minutes before and after rolling. This relaxes the gluten (protein) in the flour and helps avoid shrinkage during baking.

ROLLING

Roll pastry evenly on a lightly floured surface or between sheets of baking paper, greaseproof paper or plastic wrap. Start rolling from the centre outwards, each time, rolling the pastry towards you then away from you. Reduce the pressure towards the edges; do not roll over the edges. If rolling on a surface such as timber, marble etc., keep turning the pastry to ensure it does not stick to the surface. Use only enough flour to prevent dough sticking; excess flour upsets the balance of the ingredients. Pastry is best rolled on a cold surface; marble is perfect, but use what you've got. Short, light strokes with the rolling pin will give best results.

LINING A DISH WITH PASTRY

Place pastry over rolling pin and carefully lift pastry into the flan tin, pie plate or dish. Gently ease pastry into tin, taking care not to stretch the pastry. Gently ease the pastry over the base and side, pressing gently against the surface of the tin to avoid air pockets.

BAKING BLIND

Cut a sheet of baking paper about 5cm larger than flan tin, pie plate or dish. Cover pastry with paper, fill with dried beans or rice, or small metal disks or small ceramic balls, available from kitchen specialty shops. Place on oven tray, bake in moderately hot oven 10 minutes or as specified. Remove paper and beans carefully from pastry case, bake further 10 minutes or until golden; cool.

When beans or rice are cold, store them in an airtight container for future use for baking blind, as this procedure is called.

STORING AND FREEZING

Pastry can be stored, wrapped securely in plastic, in the refrigerator for one to two days, or frozen for up to two months. Ensure frozen pastry is at room temperature before rolling out to required size.

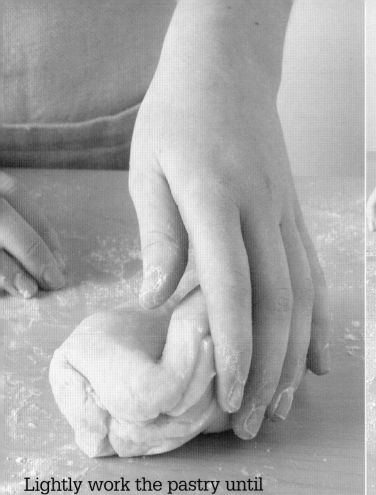

Lightly work the pastry until dough is a manageable shape.

To roll pastry, start in centre and roll pastry towards and away from you.

Place the pastry over rolling pin and carefully lift into prepared pan.

Use a knife to cleanly trim the edges of the pastry shell.

PREPARATION TIME 50 MINUTES
(PLUS REFRIGERATION TIME)
COOKING TIME 50 MINUTES
(PLUS COOLING TIME)

old-fashioned apple pie

1 cup (150g) plain flour

½ cup (75g) self-raising flour

¼ cup (35g) cornflour

¼ cup (30g) custard powder

2 tablespoons caster sugar

125g cold butter, chopped

1 egg, separated

¼ cup (60ml) iced water, approximately

LEMONY APPLE FILLING

7 large apples (1.5kg)

½ cup (125ml) water

2 tablespoons sugar

¼ teaspoon ground cinnamon

1 teaspoon grated lemon rind

TIP This apple pie can be made two days ahead and refrigerated, covered, but pastry will tend to soften a little under the apple.

1 Make lemony apple filling.

2 Blend or process flours, custard powder, half the sugar and all the butter until combined. Add egg yolk and enough of the water to make ingredients just come together. Knead dough on lightly floured surface until smooth. Wrap in plastic wrap; refrigerate 30 minutes.

3 Roll two-thirds of the dough between sheets of baking paper until large enough to line 23cm-round pie dish. Ease dough into dish; trim edge. Cover; refrigerate 30 minutes.

4 Preheat oven to moderate.

5 Roll remaining pastry between sheets of baking paper until large enough to cover pie; discard pastry scraps.

6 Spoon lemony apple filling evenly into pastry case; brush edge of pastry with some of the lightly beaten egg white. Cover filling with pastry sheet. Press edges together firmly; trim using knife. Using fingers, pinch edges to make a frill. Brush pastry with a little remaining egg white. Sprinkle pie evenly with remaining sugar.

7 Bake in moderate oven 40 minutes or until pie is golden brown.

LEMONY APPLE FILLING Peel apples; cut into quarters. Remove cores; cut each quarter in half lengthways. Place apples in large saucepan with the water; bring to a boil. Reduce heat; cover. Cook about 5 minutes or until apples are just tender. Transfer apples to large bowl; gently stir in sugar, cinnamon and lemon rind. Cool to room temperature.

serves 8

rhubarb galette

PREPARATION TIME 10 MINUTES
COOKING TIME 20 MINUTES

You need about four trimmed large stems of rhubarb (250g) for this recipe.

1 Preheat oven to hot. Line oven tray with baking paper.

2 Combine butter, rhubarb, sugar and rind in medium bowl.

3 Cut 24cm round from pastry, place on prepared tray; sprinkle almond meal evenly over pastry. Spread rhubarb mixture over pastry, leaving a 4cm border. Fold 2cm of pastry edge up and around filling. Brush edge with extra butter.

4 Bake galette, uncovered, in hot oven about 20 minutes or until browned lightly.

serves 4

20g butter, melted

2½ cups (275g) coarsely chopped rhubarb

⅓ cup (75g) firmly packed brown sugar

1 teaspoon finely grated orange rind

1 sheet ready-rolled puff pastry

2 tablespoons almond meal

10g butter, melted, extra

Use only the stalks of the rhubarb, sometimes called the "pie plant" – its leaves and roots are toxic.

PREPARATION TIME 1 HOUR
COOKING TIME 20 MINUTES

fruit mince tarts

2 cups (300g) plain flour

2 tablespoons custard powder

⅓ cup (75g) caster sugar

185g cold butter, chopped

1 egg yolk

2 tablespoons cold water, approximately

1 egg white, beaten lightly

1 tablespoon sugar

FRUIT MINCE FILLING

475g jar fruit mince

2 tablespoons brandy

¼ cup (35g) glacé peaches, chopped

¼ cup (35g) glacé apricots, chopped

1 teaspoon grated orange rind

2 teaspoons grated lemon rind

TIP Tarts can be made three days ahead; keep, covered, in refrigerator. Reheat in moderate oven about 5 minutes.

1 Grease two 12-hole deep patty pan trays.

2 Blend or process flour, custard powder, sugar and butter until combined. Add egg yolk and enough of the water to make ingredients just come together. Knead dough on lightly floured surface until smooth. Cover in plastic wrap; refrigerate 30 minutes.

3 Roll two-thirds of the dough between sheets of baking paper until 3mm thick. Cut 24 x 7.5cm rounds from pastry, re-roll pastry if necessary to make 24 rounds. Place rounds into greased trays, reserve the pastry scraps. Cover, refrigerate while preparing the filling.

4 Prepare fruit mince filling.

5 Preheat oven to moderately hot.

6 Spoon 1 heaped teaspoon of fruit mince into pastry cases. Roll remaining pastry until 3mm thick. Using 4.5cm star and Christmas tree cutters, cut out 12 stars and 12 trees. Place pastry shapes in centre of tarts; brush with egg white, sprinkle with sugar.

7 Bake in moderately hot oven about 20 minutes or until browned lightly.

FRUIT MINCE FILLING Combine ingredients in medium bowl.

makes 24

lemon meringue pie

PREPARATION TIME 45 MINUTES
(PLUS REFRIGERATION TIME)
COOKING TIME 25 MINUTES
(PLUS COOLING TIME)

1 Blend or process flour, sugar and butter until combined. Add egg yolks and enough of the water to make ingredients just come together. Knead dough on lightly floured surface until smooth. Wrap in plastic wrap; refrigerate 30 minutes.

2 Roll dough between sheets of baking paper until large enough to line 24cm-round loose-based flan tin. Ease dough into tin, trim edge. Lightly prick pastry with fork, cover, refrigerate 30 minutes.

3 Meanwhile, make lemon filling.

4 Preheat oven to moderately hot.

5 Place tin on oven tray. Line pastry case with baking paper, fill with dried beans or rice. Bake, uncovered, in moderately hot oven 10 minutes. Remove paper and beans; bake, uncovered, in moderately hot oven about 10 minutes or until browned; cool to room temperature.

6 Reduce oven to moderate.

7 Spread filling into pastry case, top with meringue; spread meringue to edge of pastry. Bake in moderate oven about 5 minutes or until meringue is browned lightly. Stand 5 minutes before serving.

LEMON FILLING Combine cornflour and sugar in medium saucepan, gradually blend in juice and the water; stir until smooth. Stir over heat until mixture boils and thickens (mixture should be very thick). Reduce heat, simmer, stirring vigorously, for 30 seconds. Remove from heat, quickly stir in rind, yolks and butter. Stir until butter is melted; cover, cool.

MERINGUE Beat egg whites in small bowl with electric mixer until soft peaks form, add cream of tartar. Gradually add sugar, beat until dissolved between additions.

serves 8

1 cup (150g) plain flour

¼ cup (55g) caster sugar

60g cold butter, chopped

2 egg yolks

2 teaspoons iced water, approximately

LEMON FILLING

½ cup (75g) cornflour

1 cup (220g) caster sugar

½ cup (125g) lemon juice

1¼ cups (310ml) water

2 teaspoons grated lemon rind

3 egg yolks

60g butter

MERINGUE

4 egg whites

pinch cream of tartar

½ cup (110g) caster sugar

TIPS Uncooked rice or dried beans used to weigh down the pastry during blind-baking are not suitable for eating. Reuse them every time you bake-blind; after cooling, keep in an airtight jar.
Pastry case and filling can be made a day ahead. Meringue is best made just before serving.
Store pastry case, in airtight container, keep filling, covered, in the refrigerator.

PREPARATION TIME 20 MINUTES
COOKING TIME 40 MINUTES

roasted pear tart

3 medium pears (700g)

1 tablespoon maple syrup

¼ cup (55g) raw sugar

40g butter, chopped

1 sheet ready rolled butter-puff pastry

1 egg, beaten lightly

TIPS Pears can be roasted several hours ahead. Tart is best cooked close to serving. Serve with ice-cream or hot custard.

1 Preheat oven to moderate.

2 Peel pears, leaving stems intact; cut in half lengthways. Remove cores carefully. Place pears in baking dish, cut-side up; top with syrup, sugar and butter.

3 Bake pears in moderate oven about 20 minutes or until tender, brushing pears occasionally with pan juices and turning the pears over after 10 minutes.

4 Increase oven temperature moderately hot.

5 Cut pastry sheet in half; place pastry halves about 2cm apart on greased oven tray.

6 Place 3 pear halves, cut-side down, on each pastry half. Brush pears and pastry with reserved syrup, then brush pastry only with a little of the egg.

7 Bake in moderately hot oven about 20 minutes or until pastry puffed and browned lightly. To serve, cut pastry so each serving contains a pear half.

serves 6

Golden, glazed pears on a simple pastry base.

palmiers

PREPARATION TIME 15 MINUTES
(PLUS REFRIGERATION TIME)
COOKING TIME 20 MINUTES

These traditional Parisian specialties are named after a palm tree because, when baked, they resemble palm fronds. Quick and easy, they're great for afternoon tea.

2 tablespoons caster sugar, approximately

2 sheets ready-rolled puff pastry, thawed

1 Sprinkle surface with a little sugar. Using rolling pin press pastry gently into sugar. Fold two opposing sides of pastry inwards to meet in the middle. Sprinkle with a little more sugar, fold in half again so edges just touch in the middle; flatten slightly. Repeat process with remaining pastry and sugar; cover, refrigerate 30 minutes.

2 Meanwhile, preheat oven to moderately hot.

3 Cut pastry roll into 1.5cm slices; place slices about 10cm apart on lightly greased oven trays.

4 Bake in moderately hot oven 10 minutes. Turn palmiers with eggslice; bake further 10 minutes or until crisp. Lift onto wire racks to cool.

makes 32

TIPS Palmiers can be made two days ahead; keep, covered, in an airtight container. Uncooked palmiers are suitable to freeze.

PREPARATION TIME 45 MINUTES

COOKING TIME 45 MINUTES

(PLUS COOLING TIME)

apple cream pie

2 medium green apples (300g),
peeled, sliced thinly

2 eggs

½ cup (110g) caster sugar

2 tablespoons plain flour

2 teaspoons grated lemon rind

1¾ cups (425ml) cream

250g packaged cream cheese, softened

1 tablespoon mixed peel

¼ cup (40g) raisins, chopped finely

1 teaspoon ground cinnamon

PASTRY

1¼ cups (185g) plain flour

½ teaspoon ground cinnamon

¼ cup (55g) caster sugar

1 teaspoon baking powder

2 teaspoons grated lemon rind

125g cold butter, chopped coarsely

1 egg yolk

2 tablespoons dry sherry

1 Preheat oven to moderate. Make pastry.

2 Arrange apple in overlapping lines in pastry case. Beat eggs and sugar in small bowl with electric mixer until thick; gradually add flour, beating well between additions. Add rind, ½ cup (125ml) of the cream, cream cheese, peel and raisins; mix well.

3 Pour filling over apples; bake in moderate oven 45 minutes; cool.

4 Beat remaining cream; spread evenly over top of pie. Sprinkle with cinnamon.

PASTRY Combine flour, cinnamon, sugar, baking powder and rind in medium bowl; rub in butter. Beat egg yolk and sherry in small bowl until combined. Add to flour mixture; mix well. Spread dough evenly over base of 19cm x 29cm rectangular slice pan.

serves 10

TIP Pie can be made up to two days ahead; keep, covered, in refrigerator.

Easy and inexpensive to make, and terrific for a crowd.

nectarine and macadamia tart

PREPARATION TIME 30 MINUTES
(PLUS REFRIGERATION TIME)
COOKING TIME 1 HOUR
(PLUS COOLING TIME)

1 Blend or process flour, sugar and butter until combined. Add egg yolk, extract and enough of the water to make ingredients just come together. Knead dough on lightly floured surface until smooth. Wrap in plastic wrap; refrigerate 30 minutes.

2 Roll dough between sheets of baking paper until large enough to line the base and side of 24cm-round, loose-based flan tin. Ease dough into tin; trim edge. Place flan tin on oven tray; cover, refrigerate 30 minutes.

3 Meanwhile, preheat oven to moderate.

4 Line pastry case with baking paper, fill with dried beans or rice. Bake, uncovered, in moderate oven 20 minutes. Remove paper and beans; bake, uncovered, in moderate oven about 5 minutes or until browned lightly.

5 Meanwhile, make macadamia filling.

6 Spread macadamia filling into pastry case; arrange nectarine segments over filling. Bake in moderate oven about 35 minutes or until golden brown and firm to touch. Cool.

MACADAMIA FILLING Process macadamias and 2 tablespoons of the flour until fine. Beat butter and sugar in small bowl with electric mixer until pale. Beat in egg and egg yolk until combined, then fold in syrup, macadamia mixture and remaining flour.

serves 8

1¼ cups (185g) plain flour

2 tablespoons caster sugar

90g cold butter, chopped

1 egg yolk

½ teaspoon vanilla extract

2 teaspoons cold water, approximately

3 medium nectarines (500g), cut into eighths

MACADAMIA FILLING

¾ cup (110g) macadamias

¼ cup (35g) plain flour

75g butter

⅓ cup (75g) firmly packed brown sugar

1 egg

1 egg yolk

2 tablespoons maple syrup

TIPS Serve tart dusted with sifted icing sugar, if desired.

Recipe can be made up to two days ahead; keep, covered, in refrigerator.

PREPARATION TIME 30 MINUTES
COOKING TIME 45 MINUTES
(PLUS COOLING TIME)

2 x 825g cans dark plums in light syrup

2 cups (300g) dried apricots

1 cinnamon stick

3 cloves

½ teaspoon mixed spice

½ teaspoon ground ginger

2 sheets ready-rolled puff pastry

1 egg, beaten lightly

SPICED YOGURT CREAM

½ cup (140g) yogurt

½ cup (120g) sour cream

1 tablespoon ground cinnamon

¼ teaspoon ground ginger

icing sugar mixture, for dusting

TIP Pie can be made a day ahead; keep, covered, in refrigerator.

spiced apricot and plum pie

1 Preheat oven to moderately hot. Grease 26cm pie dish or deep 1.25 litre (5-cup) rectangular dish.

2 Drain plums, reserve 1 cup of the syrup.

3 Halve plums, discard stones, place plums in prepared dish. Combine reserved syrup, apricots, cinnamon, cloves, mixed spice and ginger in medium saucepan, simmer, uncovered, until liquid is reduced to ½ cup. Remove and discard cinnamon stick and cloves; cool to room temperature. Pour mixture over plums.

4 Cut pastry into 2.5cm strips. Brush edge of dish with some of the egg; press pastry strips around edge of dish. Twist remaining strips, place over filling in a lattice pattern; trim ends, brush top with remaining egg.

5 Bake pie in moderately hot oven about 40 minutes or until pastry is browned lightly. Dust pie generously with icing sugar and serve with spiced yogurt cream.

SPICED YOGURT CREAM Combine ingredients in small bowl.

serves 8

A deep-dish pie with generous helpings of fruit
– perfect after a Sunday roast.

lemon tart

PREPARATION TIME 30 MINUTES
(PLUS REFRIGERATION TIME)
COOKING TIME 55 MINUTES
(PLUS COOLING TIME)

You need about three medium lemons (420g) for this tart.

1 Blend or process flour, icing sugar, almond meal and butter until combined. Add egg yolk, process until ingredients just come together. Knead dough on lightly floured surface until smooth. Wrap in plastic wrap, refrigerate 30 minutes.

2 Roll pastry between sheets of baking paper until large enough to line 24cm-round loose-based flan tin. Ease dough into tin; trim edge. Cover; refrigerate 30 minutes.

3 Meanwhile, preheat oven to moderately hot.

4 Place tin on oven tray. Line pastry case with baking paper, fill with dried beans or rice. Bake, uncovered, in moderately hot oven 15 minutes. Remove paper and beans; bake, uncovered, in moderately hot oven about 10 minutes or until browned lightly.

5 Meanwhile, make lemon filling.

6 Reduce oven to moderate.

7 Pour lemon filling into pastry case, bake in moderate oven about 30 minutes or until filling has set slightly; cool.

8 Refrigerate until cold. Serve dusted with sifted icing sugar, if desired.

LEMON FILLING Whisk ingredients in medium bowl; stand 5 minutes.

serves 8

1¼ cups (185g) plain flour

¼ cup (40g) icing sugar mixture

¼ cup (30g) almond meal

125g cold butter, chopped

1 egg yolk

LEMON FILLING

1 tablespoon finely grated lemon rind

½ cup (125ml) lemon juice

5 eggs

¾ cup (165g) caster sugar

1 cup (250ml) thickened cream

TIP This tart tastes even better if made the day before required; keep, covered, in refrigerator.

PREPARATION TIME 20 MINUTES
(PLUS REFRIGERATION TIME)
COOKING TIME 45 MINUTES

1¼ cups (185g) plain flour

⅓ cup (55g) icing sugar mixture

¼ cup (30g) almond meal

125g cold butter, chopped

1 egg yolk

FILLING

⅓ cup (50g) macadamias, toasted

⅓ cup (45g) pecans, toasted

⅓ cup (35g) walnuts, toasted

2 tablespoons brown sugar

1 tablespoon plain flour

40g butter, melted

2 eggs, beaten lightly

¾ cup (180ml) maple syrup

TIPS Do not use maple-flavoured syrup as a substitute for the "real thing" in the nut filling.

To toast nuts, place in a heavy-based frying pan, stir nuts constantly over medium-to-high heat, until they are evenly browned. Remove from pan immediately.

mini pecan, macadamia and walnut pies

1 Grease four 10cm-round loose-based flan tins.

2 Blend or process flour, icing sugar, almond meal and butter until combined. Add egg yolk; process until ingredients just come together. Knead dough on lightly floured surface until smooth. Wrap in plastic wrap, refrigerate 30 minutes.

3 Divide pastry into quarters. Roll each piece, between sheets of baking paper, into rounds large enough to line prepared tins; lift pastry into each tin. Press into sides; trim edges. Cover; refrigerate 30 minutes.

4 Meanwhile, preheat oven to moderately hot.

5 Place tins on oven tray. Line each tin with baking paper, fill with dried beans or rice. Bake, uncovered, in moderately hot oven 10 minutes. Remove paper and beans. Bake, uncovered, in moderately hot oven about 7 minutes or until pastry cases are browned lightly.

6 Reduce oven temperature to moderate.

7 Divide filling among cases. Bake in moderate oven about 25 minutes or until set; cool.

FILLING Combine ingredients in medium bowl; mix well.

serves 4

blackberry and apple pie

PREPARATION TIME 50 MINUTES
(PLUS REFRIGERATION TIME)
COOKING TIME 1 HOUR 10 MINUTES
(PLUS COOLING TIME)

1 Peel and core apples; slice thinly. Place in large saucepan with caster sugar; cook, covered, over low heat, about 10 minutes or until apples are just tender. Strain over small saucepan; reserve cooking liquid.

2 Blend cornflour with the water, stir into reserved cooking liquid over heat until mixture boils and thickens. Place apples in large bowl, gently stir in cornflour mixture; cool to room temperature.

3 Meanwhile, make pastry.

4 Preheat oven to hot.

5 Toss blackberries in extra cornflour; stir gently into apple mixture.

6 Spoon fruit mixture into pastry case; top with rolled pastry. Press edges together, trim with knife; decorate edge. Brush pastry with a little water; sprinkle with demerara sugar. Using knife, make three cuts in top of pastry to allow steam to escape.

7 Place pie on oven tray; bake, uncovered, in hot oven 20 minutes. Reduce oven temperature to moderately hot; bake, uncovered, in moderately hot oven about 30 minutes or until pastry is browned lightly. Cool 10 minutes before serving.

PASTRY Blend or process flour, icing sugar and butter until combined. Add egg yolks and enough of the water to make ingredients just come together. Knead dough on lightly floured surface until smooth. Wrap in plastic wrap, refrigerate 30 minutes. Roll two-thirds of the dough between sheets of baking paper until large enough to line 23cm-round pie dish. Ease dough into dish; trim edge. Cover; refrigerate 30 minutes. Roll remaining pastry between sheets of baking paper until large enough to cover pie.

serves 8

9 medium apples (1.5kg)

2 tablespoons caster sugar

1 tablespoon cornflour

1 tablespoon water

300g frozen blackberries

1 tablespoon cornflour, extra

1 tablespoon demerara sugar

PASTRY

2 cups (300g) plain flour

⅔ cup (110g) icing sugar mixture

185g cold butter, chopped

2 egg yolks

1 tablespoon iced water, approximately

TIPS We used golden delicious apples in this recipe.
For a different flavour, replace blackberries with blueberries, raspberries or strawberries.
This recipe is best made on the day of serving.

Friands

1 almond friands

PREPARATION TIME 20 MINUTES
COOKING TIME 25 MINUTES

Friands gain their texture from the icing sugar and almond meal that partly replaces flour.

6 egg whites
185g butter, melted
1 cup (125g) almond meal
1½ cups (240g) icing sugar mixture
½ cup (75g) plain flour

1 Preheat oven to moderately hot. Grease 12 x ⅓-cup (125ml) pans; stand on oven tray.

2 Place egg whites in medium bowl; whisk lightly with fork until combined. Add remaining ingredients to bowl. Using wooden spoon, stir until just combined. (To add flavour variations, see right.)

3 Divide mixture among prepared pans.

4 Bake in moderately hot oven about 25 minutes. Stand 5 minutes then turn onto wire rack. Serve dusted with extra sifted icing sugar, if desired.

makes 12

TIPS If using frozen berries, use them unthawed to minimise their colour "bleeding" into the mixture.
You can use frozen egg whites, thawed, in these recipes. These are readily available in supermarkets.
Friands are at their best made on the day of serving, but can be stored in an airtight container for two days, or frozen for up to three months.
Frozen friands can be thawed, individually wrapped in foil, in a moderate oven for about 15 minutes or in a microwave oven, unwrapped, on HIGH (100%) for about 30 seconds.
This basic mixture will also fill 9 x ½-cup (125ml) oval friand pan or 8 x ½-cup (125ml) rectangular friand pan.

variations

These variations are added to the basic almond friand mixture.

2 **RASPBERRY AND WHITE CHOCOLATE** Stir 100g coarsely chopped white chocolate into the egg-white mixture. Top friands with 100g fresh or frozen raspberries.

3 **LIME COCONUT** Stir 2 teaspoons finely grated lime rind, 1 tablespoon lime juice and ¼ cup (20g) desiccated coconut into the egg-white mixture; sprinkle unbaked friands with ⅓ cup (15g) flaked coconut.

4 **PASSIONFRUIT** Use hazelnut or almond meal. Drizzle the pulp of two medium passionfruit over unbaked friands.

5 **BERRY** Top unbaked friands with 100g fresh or frozen mixed berries.

6 **CITRUS AND POPPY SEED** Add two teaspoons grated lemon or orange rind and one tablespoon poppy seeds to the egg-white mixture.

7 **CHOCOLATE AND HAZELNUT** Replace almond meal with hazelnut meal. Stir 100g coarsely chopped dark chocolate into egg-white mixture. Sprinkle unbaked friands with ¼ cup coarsely chopped hazelnuts.

8 **PLUM** Use hazelnut or almond meal. Top unbaked friands with 2 medium (200g) thinly sliced plums.

1

2

3

4

any one of
these delicious
friands will go
perfectly with
your morning
cup of coffee

5

6

7

8

Biscuits

beautiful biscuits

OVEN TRAYS

We used aluminium oven trays with no sides, or very shallow sides, so the heat of the oven can circulate freely around the biscuits. Grease trays lightly.

OVEN POSITION

Two or more trays of biscuits can be cooked at the same time, provided the trays don't touch the oven walls or door. Leave a 2cm space around each tray to allow for proper heat circulation and browning. During cooking time, swap and rotate the position of trays or pans on the oven shelves – some ovens have hot spots and rotating the trays ensures even browning. Fan-forced ovens brown evenly – there's no need to swap the position of trays in a fan-forced oven.

MIXING

For best results, have all ingredients at room temperature, unless recipe indicates otherwise.

Do not overbeat butter and sugar mixture, as this results in a mixture that is excessively soft, causing the biscuits to spread too much while they are baking.

TESTING BISCUITS

The cooking times in this book are to be used as a guide only, as times vary from oven to oven. Biscuits generally feel soft in the oven and become firmer when cold.

To test if a biscuit is cooked, push it gently with your finger; if it can be moved on the oven tray without breaking, it is cooked.

STORING AND FREEZING BISCUITS

To prevent biscuits from softening, completely cool them before storing. Keep biscuits in an airtight container just large enough to hold them. Biscuits with cream or jam fillings are best assembled on day of serving.

To freeze unbaked biscuits, place scoops of biscuit dough on baking-paper-lined oven trays; freeze until firm, then transfer to an airtight container, placing sheets of baking paper between layers.

To freeze uniced or unfilled baked biscuits, place cooled biscuits in an airtight container, using sheets of baking paper between layers.

To re-crisp cookies that have gone a little stale, place on a lightly greased oven tray and bake in a slow oven for about 10 minutes.

Do not overbeat; the mixture should be pale and fluffy (top).

Leave a space between biscuits to allow for expansion during cooking.

To test if the biscuit is cooked, gently push it with your thumb.

Some ovens have hot spots. Rotating the trays prevents overbrowning.

pistachio shortbread mounds

PREPARATION TIME 25 MINUTES
COOKING TIME 25 MINUTES PER TRAY
(PLUS COOLING TIME)

½ cup (75g) shelled pistachios

250g butter, chopped

1 cup (160g) icing sugar mixture

1½ cups (225g) plain flour

2 tablespoons rice flour

2 tablespoons cornflour

¾ cup (90g) almond meal

⅓ cup (55g) icing sugar mixture, extra

TIPS Rice flour, also known as ground rice, is a very fine powder made from pulverised long-grain or glutinous rice.
Store biscuits in an airtight container for up to two weeks.
Suitable to freeze for up to three months.

1 Preheat oven to slow.

2 Toast nuts in small heavy-based frying pan until lightly browned; remove from pan. Coarsely chop ⅓ cup (50g) of the nuts; leave remaining nuts whole.

3 Beat butter and sifted icing sugar in small bowl with electric mixer until light and fluffy; transfer mixture to large bowl. Stir in sifted flours, almond meal and chopped nuts.

4 Shape level tablespoons of mixture into mounds; place mounds on lightly greased oven trays, allowing 3cm between each mound. Press one reserved nut on each mound; bake in slow oven about 25 minutes or until firm. Stand mounds on tray 5 minutes; transfer to wire rack to cool. Serve mounds dusted with extra sifted icing sugar.

makes 40

A triple-textured, mouth-watering morsel.

orange coconut
and almond biscotti

PREPARATION TIME 25 MINUTES
COOKING TIME 1 HOUR (PLUS COOLING TIME)

1 Preheat oven to moderate.

2 Whisk sugar, eggs and rind together in medium bowl. Stir in sifted flours, coconut and nuts; mix to a sticky dough.

3 Knead dough on lightly floured surface until smooth. Divide dough into two portions. Using floured hands, roll each portion into a 20cm log; place logs on lightly greased oven tray.

4 Bake in moderate oven about 35 minutes or until browned lightly. Cool on tray 10 minutes.

5 Reduce oven to moderately slow.

6 Using a serrated knife, cut logs diagonally into 1cm slices. Place slices, in single layer, on ungreased oven trays.

7 Bake in moderately slow oven about 25 minutes or until dry and crisp, turning over halfway through cooking; cool on wire racks.

makes 30

1 cup (220g) caster sugar

2 eggs

1 teaspoon grated orange rind

1⅓ cups (200g) plain flour

⅓ cup (50g) self-raising flour

⅔ (50g) shredded coconut

1 cup (160g) blanched almonds

TIPS Store biscotti in an airtight container for up to four weeks. Not suitable to freeze.

Have on hand for afternoon tea; dish up with gelato or serve with a dessert wine.

PREPARATION TIME 15 MINUTES

COOKING TIME 45 MINUTES PER TRAY

(PLUS COOLING TIME)

coconut macaroons

1 egg, separated

1 egg yolk

¼ cup (55g) caster sugar

1⅔ cups (120g) shredded coconut

1 Preheat oven to slow.

2 Beat egg yolks and sugar in small bowl until creamy; stir in coconut.

3 Beat egg white in small bowl until firm peaks form; stir gently into coconut mixture.

4 Drop heaped teaspoons of the mixture onto greased oven trays.

5 Bake in slow oven 15 minutes. Reduce heat to very slow; bake further 30 minutes or until biscuits are golden brown; loosen biscuits, cool on trays.

TIPS Store biscuits in an airtight container for up to three weeks.
Suitable to freeze for up to three months.

makes 18

A little treat that's hard to beat for a companion to coffee.

macadamia shortbread

PREPARATION TIME 20 MINUTES
COOKING TIME 20 MINUTES PER TRAY
(PLUS COOLING TIME)

1 Preheat oven to moderately slow.

2 Beat butter, sugar and extract in small bowl with electric mixer until pale and fluffy. Transfer mixture to large bowl; stir in sifted flours and nuts in two batches. Press ingredients together. Turn onto lightly floured surface; knead until smooth (do not over knead).

3 Divide mixture into two portions. Roll each portion, between two sheets of baking paper, into 23cm circle. Press an upturned 22cm loose-based fluted flan tin into shortbread to cut rounds. Cut each round into 12 wedges. Place on lightly greased oven trays; mark with a fork, sprinkle with extra sugar.

4 Bake in moderately slow oven about 20 minutes or until a pale straw colour. Stand on tray 10 minutes before transferring to wire rack to cool.

makes 24

250g butter, chopped

½ cup (110g) caster sugar

2 teaspoons vanilla extract

2 cups (300g) plain flour

½ cup (75g) rice flour

½ cup (75g) finely chopped macadamias

2 tablespoons caster sugar, extra

TIPS Store biscuits in an airtight container for up to three weeks. Suitable to freeze for up to three months.

This elegant biscuit is a perfect partner to a cup of tea or as part of a platter of fruit, cheese and chocolate.

PREPARATION TIME 20 MINUTES

COOKING TIME 15 MINUTES PER TRAY

(PLUS COOLING TIME)

lemon shortbreads

250g butter, chopped

1 teaspoon finely grated lemon rind

⅓ cup (55g) icing sugar mixture

1½ cups (225g) plain flour

½ cup (75g) cornflour

½ cup (85g) mixed peel, chopped finely

1 Preheat oven to moderate.

2 Beat butter, rind and sifted icing sugar in small bowl with electric mixer until just changed in colour. Stir in sifted flours in two batches.

3 Place mixture into large piping bag fitted with fluted tube, pipe mixture into rosettes, about 2cm apart, onto lightly greased oven trays; sprinkle with mixed peel.

4 Bake in moderate oven about 15 minutes or until browned lightly. Stand on tray 10 minutes before transferring to wire rack to cool.

makes 40

TIPS Store biscuits in an airtight container for up to three weeks. Suitable to freeze for up to three months.

A dainty shortbread with a citrus twist.

kisses

PREPARATION TIME 25 MINUTES
COOKING TIME 10 MINUTES PER TRAY
(PLUS COOLING TIME)

1 Preheat oven to moderately hot.

2 Beat butter and sugar in small bowl with electric mixer until smooth and creamy; add egg, beat only until combined. Stir in sifted dry ingredients in two batches.

3 Spoon mixture into piping bag fitted with 1cm tube. Pipe mixture into 3cm-diameter rounds, about 3cm apart, onto lightly greased oven trays.

4 Bake in moderately hot oven about 10 minutes or until browned lightly. Loosen biscuits, cool on trays.

5 Sandwich cold biscuits with vienna cream; dust with a little extra sifted icing sugar, if desired.

VIENNA CREAM Beat butter in small bowl with electric mixture until as white as possible. Gradually beat in half the sifted icing sugar, then milk; gradually beat in remaining icing sugar.

makes 20

125g butter

½ cup (110g) caster sugar

1 egg

⅓ cup (50g) plain flour

¼ cup (35g) self-raising flour

⅔ cup (100g) cornflour

¼ cup (30g) custard powder

VIENNA CREAM

60g butter

¾ cup (120g) icing sugar mixture

2 teaspoons milk

TIPS Store kisses in an airtight container for up to three days. Unfilled kisses suitable to freeze for up to three months.

A pop-in-the-mouth, melt-in-the-mouth, after-dinner delight.

greek almond biscuits

3 cups (375g) almond meal

1 cup (220g) caster sugar

3 drops almond essence

3 egg whites, beaten lightly

1 cup (80g) flaked almonds

1 Preheat oven to moderate.

2 Combine almond meal, sugar and essence in large bowl. Add egg white; stir until mixture forms a firm paste.

3 Roll level tablespoons of the mixture into the flaked almonds; roll into 8cm logs. Press on any remaining almonds. Shape logs to form crescents. Place on baking-paper-lined oven trays.

4 Bake in moderate oven about 15 minutes or until browned lightly. Cool on trays.

makes 25

TIPS Store biscuits in an airtight container for up to one week. Suitable to freeze for up to three months.

Rich, moist crescents that are spectacular with sweet Greek coffee.

triple-choc cookies

PREPARATION TIME 10 MINUTES
COOKING TIME 10 MINUTES PER TRAY
(PLUS COOLING TIME)

1 Preheat oven to moderate.

2 Beat butter, extract, sugar and egg in small bowl with electric mixer until smooth; do not overbeat. Stir in sifted dry ingredients, then raisins and all the chocolate.

3 Drop level tablespoons of mixture onto lightly greased oven trays, allowing 5cm between each cookie.

4 Bake in moderate oven about 10 minutes. Stand cookies on trays 5 minutes; transfer to wire rack to cool.

makes 36

125g butter, chopped

1 teaspoon vanilla extract

1¼ cups (275g) firmly packed brown sugar

1 egg

1 cup (150g) plain flour

¼ cup (35g) self-raising flour

1 teaspoon bicarbonate of soda

⅓ cup (35g) cocoa powder

½ cup (85g) chopped raisins

½ cup (95g) milk Choc Bits

½ cup (75g) white chocolate Melts, halved

½ cup (75g) dark chocolate Melts, halved

TIPS Cookies can be stored in an airtight container for up to three weeks. Suitable to freeze for up to three months.
For a firmer cookie, bake an extra two minutes. Choc Bits hold their shape in baking, while chocolate Melts are ideal for both melting and moulding.

There have been chocoholics since ancient times when cocoa beans were currency.

mini florentines

PREPARATION TIME 10 MINUTES
COOKING TIME 6 MINUTES PER TRAY
(PLUS COOLING TIME)

¾ cup (120g) sultanas

2 cups (80g) Corn Flakes

¾ cup (60g) flaked almonds, toasted

½ cup (110g) red glacé cherries

⅔ cup (160ml) sweetened condensed milk

60g white eating chocolate, melted

60g dark eating chocolate, melted

TIPS Florentines can be stored in an airtight container for up to two weeks. Not suitable to freeze.

1 Preheat oven to moderate.

2 Combine sultanas, Corn Flakes, nuts, cherries and condensed milk in medium bowl.

3 Drop heaped teaspoons of mixture onto baking-paper-lined oven trays, allowing 5cm between each florentine.

4 Bake in moderate oven about 6 minutes or until browned lightly. Cool on trays.

5 Spread half of the bases with white chocolate and remaining half with dark chocolate; run fork through chocolate to make waves. Allow chocolate to set at room temperature.

makes 45

Quick to mix and pretty to present, these goodies inspire an afternoon tea platter.

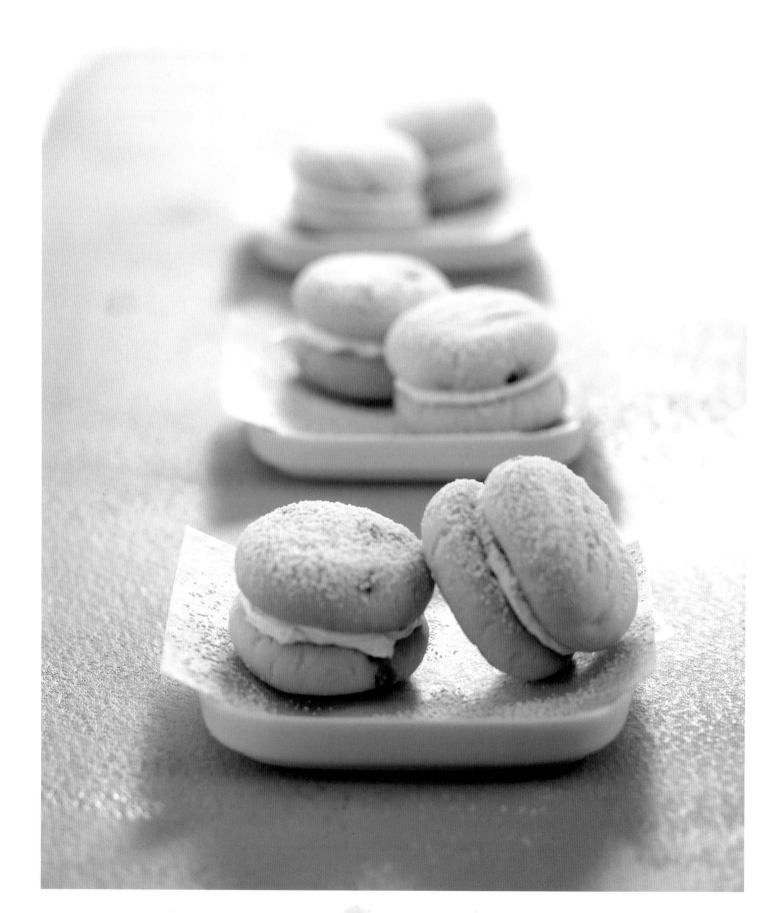

passionfruit melting moments

PREPARATION TIME 40 MINUTES
COOKING TIME 15 MINUTES PER TRAY
(PLUS COOLING TIME)

1 Preheat oven to moderately slow.

2 Remove pulp from passionfruit; place pulp into a fine sieve and press down with the back of a spoon. You will need to reserve one tablespoon of the juice for the passionfruit butter cream.

3 Beat butter, extract and sifted icing sugar with an electric mixer until pale. Stir in combined sifted flours in two batches, then stir in the passionfruit pulp.

4 With lightly floured hands, roll two level teaspoons of mixture into balls, place on baking-paper-lined oven trays about 3cm apart. Dip a fork into a little extra flour, press fork onto biscuits lightly.

5 Bake in moderately slow oven about 15 minutes or until biscuits are a pale straw colour. Stand biscuits on trays 5 minutes, transfer to wire racks to cool.

6 Sandwich biscuits with a teaspoon of the passionfruit butter cream. Dust with a little extra sifted icing sugar, if desired.

PASSIONFRUIT BUTTER CREAM Beat butter and sifted icing sugar in small bowl with an electric mixer until pale and fluffy. Beat in reserved passionfruit juice.

makes 25

3 passionfruit

250g butter, softened

1 teaspoon vanilla extract

½ cup (80g) icing sugar mixture

1⅔ cups (250g) plain flour

½ cup (75g) cornflour

PASSIONFRUIT BUTTER CREAM

80g butter, softened

⅔ cup (110g) icing sugar mixture

1 tablespoon reserved passionfruit juice

TIPS Store unfilled biscuits in an airtight container for up to two weeks. Join with passionfruit butter cream close to serving. Unfilled biscuits suitable to freeze for up to three months.

choc-hazelnut cookie sandwiches

PREPARATION TIME 25 MINUTES
(PLUS REFRIGERATION TIME)
COOKING TIME 8 MINUTES PER TRAY
(PLUS COOLING TIME)

80g butter, chopped

1 teaspoon vanilla extract

¼ cup (55g) caster sugar

1 egg

½ cup (50g) hazelnut meal

¾ cup (110g) plain flour

¼ cup (25g) cocoa powder

1 tablespoon cocoa powder, extra

CHOC-HAZELNUT CREAM

100g dark eating chocolate, melted

50g butter

⅓ cup (110g) Nutella

TIPS Store biscuits in an airtight container for up to three days. Unfilled biscuits suitable to freeze for up to three months.

1 Preheat oven to moderate.

2 Beat butter, extract, sugar and egg in small bowl with electric mixer until light and fluffy; stir in hazelnut meal, sifted flour and cocoa. Wrap dough in plastic wrap; refrigerate about 1 hour or until firm.

3 Roll dough between sheets of baking paper until 3mm thick. Using 4cm-fluted cutter, cut rounds from dough. Place rounds on lightly greased oven trays.

4 Bake in moderate oven about 8 minutes. Stand biscuits on trays 5 minutes; transfer to wire rack to cool.

5 Spoon choc-hazelnut cream into piping bag fitted with large fluted tube. Pipe cream onto one biscuit; sandwich with another biscuit. Repeat with remaining biscuits and cream. Dust with extra sifted cocoa powder.

CHOC-HAZELNUT CREAM Beat cooled chocolate, butter and Nutella in small bowl with electric mixer until thick and glossy.

makes 30

In Italy, little sandwiched biscuits are known as "lady's kisses".

anzac biscuits

PREPARATION TIME 15 MINUTES
COOKING TIME 20 MINUTES
(PLUS COOLING TIME)

1 Preheat oven to moderately slow.

2 Combine oats, sifted flour, sugar and coconut in large bowl. Combine butter, golden syrup and the water in small saucepan. Stir constantly over medium heat until butter is melted; stir in soda. Stir mixture into dry ingredients.

3 Place level tablespoons of mixture 5cm apart on lightly greased oven trays.

4 Bake in moderately slow oven about 20 minutes or until biscuits feel slightly firm. Use spatula to loosen biscuits on trays; cool on trays.

makes 30

1 cup (90g) rolled oats

1 cup (150g) plain flour

1 cup (220g) firmly packed brown sugar

½ cup (45g) desiccated coconut

125g butter

2 tablespoons golden syrup

1 tablespoon water

½ teaspoon bicarbonate of soda

TIPS Biscuits can be stored in airtight containers for up to a week. Suitable to freeze for up to three months.

An Australian tradition from great-grandmother's kitchen.

PREPARATION TIME 25 MINUTES

COOKING TIME 50 MINUTES

(PLUS COOLING TIME)

apricot and pine nut biscotti

1¼ cups (275g) caster sugar

2 eggs

1 teaspoon vanilla extract

1½ cups (225g) plain flour

½ cup (75g) self-raising flour

½ cup (125g) coarsely chopped glacé apricots

¼ cup (40g) pine nuts, toasted

2 teaspoons water

TIPS Store biscotti in an airtight container for up to four weeks. Not suitable to freeze. To toast nuts, place in a heavy-base frying pan, stir constantly over medium-to-high heat until they are evenly browned. Remove from pan immediately.

1 Preheat oven to moderate.

2 Whisk sugar, eggs and extract in medium bowl. Stir in sifted flours, apricots, pine nuts and the water; mix to a sticky dough.

3 Knead dough on lightly floured surface until smooth. Divide dough into two portions. Using floured hands, roll each portion into a 30cm log. Place logs on lightly greased oven tray.

4 Bake in moderate oven about 25 minutes or until browned lightly. Cool on tray 10 minutes.

5 Reduce oven to slow.

6 Using a serrated knife, cut logs diagonally into 1cm slices. Place slices, in single layer, on ungreased oven trays.

7 Bake in slow oven about 25 minutes or until dry and crisp, turning over halfway through cooking; cool on wire racks.

makes 50

Toasted pine nuts bring out the flavour and add contrast to the dried apricots.

choc nut biscotti

PREPARATION TIME 35 MINUTES
COOKING TIME 50 MINUTES
(PLUS COOLING TIME)

1 Preheat oven to moderate.

2 Whisk sugar and eggs in medium bowl. Stir in sifted flour, baking powder and nuts; mix to a sticky dough.

3 Knead dough on lightly floured surface until smooth. Divide dough into two portions. Using floured hands, knead one portion on lightly floured surface until smooth, but still slightly sticky. Divide this portion into four pieces.

4 Roll each piece into 25cm log shape. Knead remaining portion with cocoa until smooth, divide into two pieces. Roll each piece of chocolate mixture into a 25cm log shape.

5 Place one chocolate log on lightly greased oven tray. Place a plain log on each side, press gently together to form a slightly flattened shape. Repeat with remaining logs.

6 Bake in moderate oven about 30 minutes or until browned lightly. Cool on tray 10 minutes.

7 Reduce oven to slow.

8 Using a serrated knife, cut logs diagonally into 5mm slices. Place slices, in single layer, on ungreased oven trays.

9 Bake in slow oven about 20 minutes or until dry and crisp, turning over halfway through cooking; cool on wire racks.

makes 60

1 cup (220g) caster sugar

2 eggs

1⅔ cups (250g) plain flour

1 teaspoon baking powder

1 cup (150g) shelled pistachios, toasted

½ cup (70g) shivered almonds

¼ cup (25g) cocoa powder

TIPS Store biscotti in an airtight container for up to four weeks. Not suitable to freeze.

PREPARATION TIME 25 MINUTES
COOKING TIME 16 MINUTES PER TRAY
(PLUS COOLING TIME)

1 cup (220g) firmly packed brown sugar

½ cup (110g) caster sugar

1½ cups (225g) self-raising flour

½ cup (75g) plain flour

1 cup (150g) coarsely chopped
macadamias, toasted

185g butter, melted, cooled

1 egg, beaten lightly

1 egg yolk, beaten lightly

2 teaspoons vanilla extract

200g dark eating chocolate,
chopped coarsely

TIPS Store cookies in an airtight container
for up to two weeks. Suitable to freeze for up
to three months.

chunky chewy choc-chip cookies

We used an ice-cream scoop equivalent to two level tablespoons
when measuring the biscuit dough.

1 Preheat oven to moderate.

2 Combine sugars, sifted flours and nuts in large bowl.

3 Add combined butter, egg, egg yolk and extract; mix to a soft dough.
Stir in chocolate.

4 Place 2 level tablespoons of biscuit dough, about 6cm apart, on lightly
greased oven trays.

5 Bake in moderate oven about 16 minutes or until browned lightly. Cool
on trays.

makes 20

almond macaroons

PREPARATION TIME 20 MINUTES
COOKING TIME 10 MINUTES PER TRAY
(PLUS COOLING TIME)

1 Preheat oven to moderately slow.

2 Combine almond meal and sugar in medium bowl. Stir in combined essence and egg white; mix well.

3 Roll two level teaspoons of mixture into balls, place 3cm apart on baking-paper-lined oven trays. Place one almond on top of each macaroon and flatten slightly.

4 Bake in moderately slow oven about 10 minutes or until browned lightly. Stand on trays 5 minutes before transferring to wire rack to cool. Dust lightly with sifted icing sugar.

makes 22

1 cup (125g) almond meal

½ cup (110g) caster sugar

1 drop almond essence

1 egg white

¼ cup (40g) blanched almonds

icing sugar mixture, for dusting

TIPS Store biscuits in an airtight container for up to three weeks. Suitable to freeze for up to three months.

Sweet and cakey, with a crisp crust that forms after baking.

PREPARATION TIME 40 MINUTES
(PLUS REFRIGERATION TIME)
COOKING TIME 45 MINUTES
(PLUS COOLING TIME)

anise biscotti

125g butter

¾ cup (165g) caster sugar

3 eggs

2 tablespoons brandy

1 tablespoon grated lemon rind

1½ cups (225g) plain flour

¾ cup (110g) self-raising flour

125g blanched almonds, toasted, chopped coarsely

1 tablespoon ground aniseed

TIPS Store biscotti in an airtight container for up to four weeks. Not suitable to freeze.

1 Beat butter and sugar in large bowl with electric mixer until just combined; add eggs, one at a time, beating well after each addition. Add brandy and rind; mix well. Stir in flours, nuts and aniseed; cover, refrigerate 1 hour.

2 Preheat oven to moderate.

3 Halve dough; shape each half into a 30cm log. Place on lightly greased oven tray.

4 Bake in moderate oven about 20 minutes or until browned lightly. Cool logs on oven tray about 10 minutes.

5 Using a serrated knife, cut logs diagonally into 1cm slices. Place slices, in single layer, on ungreased oven trays.

6 Bake in moderate oven about 25 minutes or until dry and crisp, turning over halfway through cooking; cool on wire racks.

makes 40

Anise is a herb with the strong aroma and taste of liquorice.

almond jam cookies

PREPARATION TIME 35 MINUTES
COOKING TIME 25 MINUTES PER TRAY
(PLUS COOLING TIME)

1 Preheat oven to moderately slow.

2 Beat butter, extract, sugar and egg yolks in medium bowl with electric mixer until just combined.

3 Stir in almond meal, flour and baking powder; mix well. Roll level tablespoons of mixture into balls; place about 5cm apart on ungreased oven trays.

4 Press a hollow into each ball about 1 cm deep and 1.5cm wide using the handle of a lightly floured wooden spoon.

5 Combine apricot jam with half the rind. Combine raspberry jam with remaining rind. Carefully spoon a little apricot jam into half the cookies; spoon raspberry jam into remaining cookies.

6 Bake in moderately slow oven about 25 minutes or until cookies are browned lightly; cool on trays.

makes 30

185g butter, chopped

1 teaspoon vanilla extract

¾ cup (165g) caster sugar

2 egg yolks

½ cup (60g) almond meal

1½ cups (225g) plain flour

½ teaspoon baking power

2 tablespoons apricot jam, approximately

1 teaspoon grated lemon rind

2 tablespoons raspberry jam, approximately

TIPS Store cookies in an airtight container for up to three weeks. Not suitable to freeze. If jam sinks during cooking, top up with a little extra, if desired.

When you're in a jam, any jam will do.

PREPARATION TIME 25 MINUTES
(PLUS REFRIGERATION TIME)
COOKING TIME 12 MINUTES PER TRAY
(PLUS COOLING TIME)

snickerdoodles

250g butter, softened

1 teaspoon vanilla extract

½ cup (110g) firmly packed brown sugar

1 cup (220g) caster sugar

2 eggs

2¾ cups (410g) plain flour

1 teaspoon bicarbonate of soda

½ teaspoon ground nutmeg

1 tablespoon caster sugar, extra

2 teaspoons ground cinnamon

These amusingly-named cookies have a cracked surface and are rolled in cinnamon sugar before being baked. There is dispute as to the true origin of the name (most often thought to be Dutch), but we know for certain that the biscuit translates as delicious.

1 Beat butter, extract and sugars in small bowl with electric mixer until light and fluffy. Add eggs, one at a time, beating until just combined. Transfer to large bowl.

2 Stir combined sifted flour, soda and nutmeg, in two batches, into egg mixture. Cover; refrigerate dough 30 minutes.

3 Meanwhile, preheat oven to moderate.

4 Combine extra caster sugar and cinnamon in small shallow bowl. Roll level tablespoons of the dough into balls; roll balls in cinnamon sugar. Place balls on ungreased oven trays, 7cm apart.

5 Bake in moderate oven about 12 minutes. Cool biscuits on trays.

makes 50

TIPS Store biscuits in an airtight container for up to three weeks. Suitable to freeze for up to three months.

Spiced sugar cookies – this recipe makes oodles.

Slices

PREPARATION TIME 20 MINUTES
COOKING TIME 1 HOUR 5 MINUTES
(PLUS COOLING TIME)

150g butter

300g dark eating chocolate, chopped coarsely

1½ cups (330g) firmly packed brown sugar

3 eggs

2 teaspoons vanilla extract

¾ cup (110g) plain flour

¾ cup (140g) dark Choc Bits

½ cup (120g) sour cream

¾ cup (110g) macadamias, toasted, chopped coarsely

1 tablespoon cocoa powder

TIPS Store brownies in the refrigerator for up to one week.
Brownies can be light and cake-like, fudgy and dense, or moist and chewy – depending on the ratio of chocolate and butter to flour. This recipe produces a brownie that's a happy medium between fudgy and cake-like. Reduce the baking time by 10 minutes if you prefer a more moist brownie.

chocolate fudge brownies

An American classic, brownies are thought to have been "invented" by accident when a New England housewife forgot to add the baking powder to a chocolate cake she was making. Chocolate lovers around the world have enjoyed that result, in one form or another, for more than a century.

1 Preheat oven to moderate. Grease 19cm x 29cm rectangular slice pan with baking paper; line base and two long sides with baking paper, extending paper 2cm above edge of pan.

2 Melt butter in medium saucepan, add chocolate; stir over low heat, without boiling, until mixture is smooth. Stir in sugar, then transfer mixture to large bowl; cool until just warm.

3 Stir in eggs, one at a time, then stir in extract, flour, Choc Bits, cream and nuts. Spread mixture into prepared pan.

4 Bake in moderate oven about 40 minutes. Cover pan with foil, bake further 20 minutes.

5 Cool in pan; turn top-side up onto wire rack, dust with sifted cocoa. Cut into pieces before serving.

makes 12

fruity white chocolate bars

PREPARATION TIME 15 MINUTES
COOKING TIME 45 MINUTES
(PLUS COOLING TIME)

1 Preheat oven to moderately slow. Grease 19cm x 29cm rectangular slice pan; line base and two long sides with baking paper, extending paper 2cm above edge of pan.

2 Combine nuts, coconut, fruit and flour in large bowl. Stir in combined hot melted chocolate, sieved jam and honey. Spread evenly into prepared pan.

3 Bake in moderately slow oven about 45 minutes. Cool in pan before cutting into pieces.

makes 16

¾ cup (90g) slivered almonds

1¼ cups (210g) brazil nuts, coarsely chopped

1½ cups (135g) desiccated coconut

1 cup (150g) chopped dried apricots

1 cup (150g) dried currants

¼ cup (35g) plain flour

1⅔ cup (250g) white Choc Melts, melted

½ cup (160g) apricot jam

½ cup (180g) honey

TIP Store slice, covered, in refrigerator, for up to one week.

Chock full of things that are good for you... almost.

PREPARATION TIME 25 MINUTES
COOKING TIME 40 MINUTES
(PLUS COOLING TIME)

raspberry coconut slice

90g butter

½ cup (110g) caster sugar

1 egg

¼ cup (35g) self-raising flour

⅔ cup (100g) plain flour

1 tablespoon custard powder

¼ cup (80ml) raspberry jam

COCONUT TOPPING

2 eggs, beaten lightly

¼ cup (55g) caster sugar

2 cups (180g) desiccated coconut

TIP Store slice in airtight container for up to one week.

1 Preheat oven to moderate. Grease 19cm x 29cm rectangular slice pan; line base and two long sides with baking paper, extending paper 2cm above edge of pan.

2 Beat butter, sugar and egg in small bowl with electric mixer until changed to a lighter colour; stir in sifted flours and custard powder.

3 Spread mixture over base of prepared pan.

4 Bake in moderate oven 15 minutes. Stand in pan 10 minutes.

5 Spread slice base with jam, sprinkle over coconut topping.

6 Return to moderate oven; bake further 25 minutes or until browned lightly. Cool in pan before cutting.

COCONUT TOPPING Combine ingredients in medium bowl.

makes 12

A tea-time favourite through generations.

chewy chocolate slice

PREPARATION TIME 20 MINUTES
COOKING TIME 30 MINUTES
(PLUS COOLING TIME)

1 Preheat oven to moderate. Grease 19cm x 29cm rectangular slice pan; line base and two long sides with baking paper, extending paper 2cm above edge of pan.

2 Combine butter, sugar, egg and extract in medium bowl. Stir in sifted flours and cocoa powder, then coconut.

3 Spread mixture evenly over base of prepared pan.

4 Bake in moderate oven about 30 minutes or until firm.

5 Meanwhile, make chocolate icing.

6 Spread hot slice with chocolate icing; sprinkle with extra coconut. Cool in pan before cutting.

CHOCOLATE ICING Sift icing sugar and cocoa powder into medium bowl; add combined butter and water, stir until icing is a spreadable consistency.

makes 12

125g butter, melted

1 cup (220g) firmly packed brown sugar

1 egg, beaten lightly

1 teaspoon vanilla extract

½ cup (75g) plain flour

¼ cup (35g) self-raising flour

2 tablespoons cocoa powder

½ cup (45g) desiccated coconut

1 tablespoon desiccated coconut, extra

CHOCOLATE ICING

1 cup (160g) icing sugar mixture

2 tablespoons cocoa powder

10g butter, melted

1½ tablespoons hot water, approximately

TIP Store slice in an airtight container for up to one week.

A family favourite becomes a dinner-party dessert with a dollop of cream and a scattering of berries.

PREPARATION TIME 15 MINUTES

COOKING TIME 40 MINUTES

(PLUS COOLING TIME)

fruit chews

⅓ cup (75g) firmly packed brown sugar

90g butter

1¼ cups (185g) plain flour

1 egg yolk

TOPPING

2 eggs

1 cup (220g) firmly packed brown sugar

⅓ cup (50g) self-raising flour

½ cup (85g) raisins

¾ cup (120g) sultanas

1¼ cups (185g) roasted unsalted peanuts

1 cup (90g) desiccated coconut

TIP Store slice in an airtight container for up to one week.

1 Preheat oven to moderate. Grease 20cm x 30cm lamington pan; line base and two long sides with baking paper, extending paper 2cm above edge of pan.

2 Combine sugar and butter in medium saucepan; stir over medium heat until butter is melted.

3 Stir in the sifted flour and egg yolk. Press mixture over base of prepared pan.

4 Bake in moderate oven about 10 minutes or until browned lightly; cool.

5 Spread topping over cold base; return to moderate oven, bake further 30 minutes or until browned lightly. Cool in pan before cutting.

TOPPING Beat eggs and sugar in small bowl with electric mixer until changed to a lighter colour and thickened slightly; fold in sifted flour. Transfer mixture to large bowl, stir in remaining ingredients.

makes 18

Brown sugar gives this nutty slice the colour and taste of caramel.

marmalade almond squares

PREPARATION TIME 30 MINUTES
COOKING TIME 35 MINUTES
(PLUS COOLING TIME)

1 Preheat oven to moderately hot. Grease 19cm x 29cm rectangular slice pan; line base and two long sides with baking paper, extending paper 2cm above edge of pan.

2 Beat butter, essence and sugar in small bowl with electric mixer until smooth. Stir in flour and desiccated coconut; press into prepared pan.

3 Bake in moderately hot oven about 15 minutes or until browned lightly. Meanwhile, make topping.

4 Reduce oven temperature to moderate.

5 Spread hot slice with topping; sprinkle with flaked coconut.

6 Bake in moderate oven 20 minutes or until firm. Brush hot slice with marmalade; cool in pan before cutting.

TOPPING Beat butter, rind and sugar in small bowl with electric mixer until smooth; add eggs, beat until combined (mixture will look curdled at this stage). Stir in coconut and almond meal.

makes 18

125g butter, chopped
1 teaspoon almond essence
¼ cup (55g) caster sugar
1 cup (150g) plain flour
¼ cup (20g) desiccated coconut
⅓ cup (15g) flaked coconut
¼ cup (85g) marmalade, warmed

TOPPING
90g butter, chopped
2 teaspoons grated orange rind
⅓ cup (75g) caster sugar
2 eggs
1 cup (90g) desiccated coconut
1 cup (125g) almond meal

TIP Store slice, covered, in refrigerator for up to one week.

Rich, moist layers of nuts and marmalade make this slice memorable.

PREPARATION TIME 15 MINUTES

COOKING TIME 30 MINUTES

(PLUS COOLING TIME)

apricot choc-chip muesli bars

125g butter, chopped

½ cup (110g) firmly packed brown sugar

1 tablespoon honey

2¼ cups (200g) rolled oats

¼ cup (40g) sunflower kernels

¼ cup (20g) desiccated coconut

½ teaspoon ground cinnamon

½ cup (75g) chopped dried apricots

2 tablespoons dark Choc Bits

1 Preheat oven to moderately slow. Grease 20cm x 30cm lamington pan; line base and two long sides with baking paper, extending paper 2cm above edge of pan.

2 Combine butter, sugar and honey in medium saucepan; stir over low heat until sugar is dissolved.

3 Transfer butter mixture to medium bowl; stir in oats, sunflower kernels, coconut, cinnamon and apricots.

4 Press mixture into prepared pan; sprinkle with Choc Bits.

5 Bake in moderately slow oven about 30 minutes or until browned lightly.

6 Cut into pieces while still warm; cool in pan.

makes 8

TIP Store slice in an airtight container for up to one week.

The bars you buy don't make the grade next to this home-made treat.

caramel coconut slice

PREPARATION TIME 25 MINUTES
COOKING TIME 35 MINUTES
(PLUS COOLING TIME)

1 Preheat oven to moderate. Grease 26cm x 32cm swiss roll pan; line base and two long sides with baking paper, extending paper 2cm above edge of pan.

2 Sift flours into medium bowl, stir in coconut, sugar and butter; press evenly over base of prepared pan.

3 Bake in moderate oven about 10 minutes or until lightly browned; cool.

4 Spread caramel filling evenly over base; sprinkle with coconut topping.

5 Return to moderate oven; bake 25 minutes or until topping is browned lightly; cool in pan before cutting.

CARAMEL FILLING Combine ingredients in bowl; mix well.

COCONUT TOPPING Combine ingredients in bowl; mix well.

makes 12

½ cup (75g) plain flour

½ cup (75g) self-raising flour

½ cup (45g) desiccated coconut

½ cup (110g) caster sugar

100g butter, melted

CARAMEL FILLING

395g can sweetened condensed milk

2 tablespoons golden syrup

¼ cup (55g) firmly packed brown sugar

60g butter, melted

COCONUT TOPPING

4 eggs, beaten lightly

⅔ cup (150g) caster sugar

4 cups (360g) desiccated coconut

TIP Store slice in an airtight container for up to one week.

Rich and chewy, sweet and gooey.

PREPARATION TIME 20 MINUTES
COOKING TIME 20 MINUTES
(PLUS COOLING TIME)

pepita and sesame slice

90g butter

1 teaspoon grated lemon rind

2 tablespoons caster sugar

1 egg

⅔ cup (100g) plain flour

½ cup (80g) wholemeal plain flour

½ cup (80g) unsalted pepitas, chopped coarsely

¼ cup (80g) apricot jam

2 tablespoons sesame seeds, toasted

1 Preheat oven to moderately hot. Grease 23cm-square slab pan; line base and two long sides with baking paper, extending paper 2cm above edge of pan.

2 Beat butter, rind, sugar and egg in small bowl with electric mixer until light and fluffy. Stir in sifted flours and pepitas; press mixture evenly into prepared pan.

3 Spread slice with jam; sprinkle with seeds.

4 Bake in moderately hot oven about 20 minutes or until browned lightly; cool slice in pan before cutting.

makes 16

TIP Store slice in an airtight container for up to one week.

High in fibre and fabulous with fruit.

tangy lemon squares

PREPARATION TIME 20 MINUTES
COOKING TIME 35 MINUTES
(PLUS COOLING TIME)

1 Preheat oven to moderate. Grease shallow 23cm-square pan; line base and sides of pan with baking paper, extending paper 2cm above edge of pan.

2 Beat butter and icing sugar in small bowl with electric mixer until smooth. Stir in 1 cup (150g) of the flour.

3 Press mixture evenly over base of prepared pan.

4 Bake in moderate oven about 15 minutes or until browned lightly.

5 Meanwhile, place eggs, caster sugar, remaining flour, rind and juice in bowl; whisk until combined. Pour egg mixture over hot base.

6 Return to moderate oven, bake 20 minutes or until firm. Cool in pan on a wire rack before cutting. Dust with extra sifted icing sugar, if desired.

makes 16

125g butter

¼ cup (40g) icing sugar mixture

1¼ cups (185g) plain flour

3 eggs

1 cup (220g) caster sugar

2 teaspoons finely grated lemon rind

½ cup (125ml) lemon juice

TIP Store slice, covered, in the refrigerator for up to three days.

Look for lemons that are bright and heavy – they have more juice and flavour.

Big
cakes

tips and techniques

HOW TO PREPARE A CAKE PAN

We use aluminium cake pans because they give the best cake-baking results. Cake pans made from materials with various coatings, such as non-stick, work well provided that the surface is unscratched. Pans made from tin and stainless steel do not conduct heat as evenly as aluminium does.

To grease a cake pan, use either a light, even coating of cooking-oil spray, or a pastry brush to brush melted butter or margarine evenly over the base and sides.

Sometimes recipes call for a greased and floured cake pan. Simply grease the pan evenly (melted butter is best in this case) and allow it to "set" a minute or two before sprinkling a little flour evenly over the greased area. Tap the pan several times on your bench then tip out the excess flour.

To line a cake pan with baking paper, trace around the base of the pan with a pencil onto baking paper; cut out the shape slightly inside the pencil mark, so the paper fits snugly inside the greased pan. It is not necessary to grease the baking paper once it is in position.

As a guide, cakes requiring 1 hour or longer to bake should have a baking paper "collar" extending about 5cm above the edge of the pan, to protect the top of the cake. The following method of lining round or square cake pans allows for this, using baking paper:

• For sides, cut three paper strips long enough to fit around inside of the pan and 8cm wider than the depth of the pan. Fold strips lengthways about 2cm from the edge and make short diagonal cuts about 2cm apart, up to the fold. This helps ease the paper around the curves or corners of the pan, with the cut section fitting around the base.

• Using the base of pan as a guide, cut three paper circles (or squares) as instructed previously; position in base of pan after lining sides.

TO TEST IF CAKE IS COOKED

All baking times are approximate. Check your cake just after the suggested cooking time; it should be browned and starting to shrink from the sides of the pan. Feel the top with your fingertips; it should feel firm. You may want to insert a thin skewer in the deepest part of the cake (we prefer to use a metal skewer rather than a wooden one because any mixture that adheres to it is easier to see). Gently remove the skewer; it shouldn't have any uncooked mixture clinging to it. Do not confuse cake mixture with stickiness from fruit.

COOLING A CAKE

We have suggested standing times for cakes before turning onto wire racks to cool further. The best way to do this, after standing time has elapsed, is to hold the cake pan firmly and shake it gently, thus loosening the cake from the pan. Turn the cake, upside down, onto a wire rack, then turn the cake top-side up immediately using a second rack (unless directed otherwise). Some wire racks mark the cakes, particularly soft cakes such as sponges. To prevent this, cover the rack with baking paper. Unless otherwise stated, all cakes (and slices) should be cooled to room temperature before icing or filling.

HOW TO STORE A CAKE

Make sure your cake is at room temperature before storing it in an airtight container as close in size to the cake as possible; this minimises the amount of air around the cake. For those cakes that are suitable to freeze, it is usually better to freeze them unfilled and uniced because icing often cracks during the thawing process. Wrap or seal cakes in freezer bags, expelling as much air as possible. Cakes thaw best overnight in the refrigerator. Unfilled and uniced cakes can be frozen for up to three months.

Grease cake pan with melted butter brushed evenly on base and sides.

To easily place baking-paper collar, make short cuts in bottom of paper.

Insert a thin metal skewer into the cake to test if it is cooked.

Turn the cake top-side up using a second wire rack.

PREPARATION TIME 30 MINUTES
COOKING TIME 1 HOUR 20 MINUTES
(PLUS COOLING TIME)

apple custard tea cake

200g butter, softened

½ cup (110g) caster sugar

2 eggs

1¼ cups (185g) self-raising flour

⅓ cup (40g) custard powder

2 medium green apples (300g), peeled, cored, sliced thinly

1 tablespoon butter, melted

2 teaspoons caster sugar, extra

½ teaspoon ground cinnamon

CUSTARD

2 tablespoons custard powder

¼ cup (55g) caster sugar

1 cup (250ml) milk

20g butter

2 teaspoons vanilla extract

1 Make custard.

2 Preheat oven to moderate. Grease deep 22cm-round cake pan; line base with baking paper.

3 Beat butter and sugar in small bowl with electric mixer until light and fluffy. Add eggs, one at a time, beating well between additions. Stir in sifted flour and custard powder.

4 Spread half the mixture into prepared pan, top with custard. Top custard with spoonfuls of remaining cake mixture; gently spread with spatula to completely cover custard. Arrange apples on top; brush with melted butter then sprinkle with combined extra sugar and cinnamon.

5 Bake cake in moderate oven 1¼ hours; cool in pan. Sprinkle with extra caster sugar, if desired.

CUSTARD Combine custard powder and sugar in small saucepan; gradually add milk, stirring over heat until mixture thickens slightly. Remove from heat; stir in butter and extract. Press plastic wrap over surface of custard to prevent a skin forming; cool. Whisk until smooth just before using.

serves 8

TIPS Cake is best made on day of serving; keep, covered, in refrigerator.
Suitable to freeze for up to three months.

Country cooking stands the test of time.

buttery orange cake

PREPARATION TIME 20 MINUTES
COOKING TIME 1 HOUR
(PLUS COOLING TIME)

1 Preheat oven to moderately slow. Grease deep 22cm-round cake pan; line base and side with baking paper, bringing paper 5cm above edge of pan.

2 Beat butter, rind and sugar in large bowl with electric mixer until light and fluffy. Add eggs, one at a time, beating until just combined between additions. Fold in combined sifted flours and juice in two batches. Spread mixture into prepared pan.

3 Bake cake in moderately slow oven about 1 hour. Stand cake in pan 5 minutes before turning onto wire rack to cool.

GLACE ICING Sift icing sugar into small heatproof bowl; stir in butter and juice to form a firm paste. Place bowl over small saucepan of simmering water, stir until icing is a spreadable consistency; do not overheat. Top cake with glacé icing.

serves 12

250g butter, softened

2 tablespoons finely grated orange rind

1½ cups (330g) caster sugar

4 eggs

1½ cups (225g) self-raising flour

½ cup (75g) plain flour

¾ cup (180ml) orange juice

GLACE ICING

1½ cups (240g) icing sugar mixture

1 teaspoon soft butter

2 tablespoons orange juice

TIPS This recipe can be made four days ahead; store in an airtight container at room temperature.
Uniced cake suitable to freeze for up to three months.
Icing suitable to microwave.

Orange rind delivers intense flavour and aroma to this basic butter cake.

PREPARATION TIME 15 MINUTES
COOKING TIME 1 HOUR 15 MINUTES
(PLUS COOLING TIME)

125g butter, softened

1 teaspoon vanilla extract

1¼ cups (275g) caster sugar

3 eggs

1 cup (150g) plain flour

½ cup (75g) self-raising flour

¼ teaspoon bicarbonate of soda

½ cup (125ml) milk

TIPS To give this cake a slight caramel flavour, substitute 1⅓ cups (295g) firmly packed brown sugar for the caster sugar. This cake will keep in an airtight container for up to three days. Cake can be frozen for up to three months.

cut & keep butter cake

This is an easy-to-mix, one-bowl, plain cake – and there's nothing nicer with a cuppa. Simply dust it with sifted icing sugar when serving.

1 Preheat oven to moderately slow. Grease deep 20cm-round cake pan; line base with baking paper.

2 Beat ingredients in medium bowl on low speed with electric mixer until just combined. Increase speed to medium; beat until mixture is smooth and changed to a paler colour. Pour mixture into prepared pan.

3 Bake cake in moderately slow oven about 1¼ hours. Stand cake in pan 5 minutes before turning onto wire rack; turn cake top-side up to cool. Dust cake with sifted icing sugar, if desired.

serves 10

There are few things of which we can be certain, and this cake is one.

pear and almond cake with passionfruit glaze

PREPARATION TIME 30 MINUTES
COOKING TIME 55 MINUTES
(PLUS COOLING TIME)

You will need about four passionfruit for this recipe.

1 Preheat oven to moderately slow. Grease 22cm springform tin; line base and side with baking paper.

2 Beat butter and sugar in medium bowl with electric mixer until light and fluffy. Add eggs, one at a time, beating until combined between each addition. Stir in almond meal and flour. Spread mixture into prepared tin; top with pear halves, cut-side down.

3 Bake cake in moderately slow oven about 50 minutes. Stand cake in tin 5 minutes before transferring to a serving plate. Pour passionfruit glaze over cake while still warm.

PASSIONFRUIT GLAZE Stir combined ingredients in small saucepan over heat, without boiling, until sugar dissolves. Bring to a boil; reduce heat. Simmer, uncovered, without stirring, about 2 minutes or until thickened slightly; cool.

serves 10

185g butter, softened

½ cup (110g) caster sugar

3 eggs

1½ cups (185g) almond meal

¼ cup (35g) plain flour

420g can pear halves in natural juice, drained

PASSIONFRUIT GLAZE

⅓ cup (80ml) passionfruit pulp

⅓ cup (80ml) light corn syrup

1 tablespoon caster sugar

TIPS Cake can be made a day ahead; keep, covered, in refrigerator until required. Cake is not suitable to freeze.
Cover cake with glaze on day of serving. Bring glaze to room temperature before using.

A dinner-party dessert cake for a table of 10.

PREPARATION TIME 20 MINUTES

COOKING TIME 1 HOUR 45 MINUTES

(PLUS STANDING TIME)

¾ cup (165g) caster sugar

1¼ cups (310ml) water

1 medium unpeeled orange (240g), sliced thinly

1 large unpeeled lemon (180g), sliced thinly

¼ cup (60ml) water, extra

125g butter, softened

1 tablespoon finely grated lemon rind

1 cup (220g) caster sugar, extra

3 eggs

½ cup (60g) almond meal

½ cup (75g) plain flour

½ cup (75g) self-raising flour

¾ cup (120g) polenta

⅓ cup (80g) sour cream

¼ cup (60ml) lemon juice

LEMON MASCARPONE

1 cup (250g) mascarpone cheese

2 teaspoons finely grated lemon rind

1 tablespoon lemon juice

2 tablespoons caster sugar

TIPS You'll find it best to make the citrus mixture in a large frying pan rather than a saucepan, so that the citrus slices fit in a single layer.
Cake will keep for one day in an airtight container at room temperature. Cake is not suitable to freeze.

marmalade polenta cake

This cake doesn't actually contain marmalade as an ingredient, but its artful use of citrus rind strikes a similar visual chord. It is slightly painstaking to make and difficult to slice neatly, but is well worth the effort.

1 Preheat oven to moderate. Grease deep 20cm-round cake pan; line base and side with baking paper.

2 Combine sugar and the water in large frying pan; using wooden spoon, stir over heat, without boiling, until sugar dissolves. Bring to a boil, reduce heat; simmer, without stirring, uncovered, about 5 minutes or until syrup thickens slightly. Add orange and lemon slices; simmer gently, uncovered, about 7 minutes or until rind is tender, turning slices halfway through cooking time.

3 Remove syrup mixture from heat. Using tongs, lift alternate orange and lemon slices directly from syrup to cover base and side of prepared pan. Reserve syrup.

4 Add the extra water to reserved syrup in pan; bring to a boil. Reduce heat; simmer, uncovered, without stirring, about 5 minutes or until syrup is a light honey colour. Pour hot syrup over orange and lemon slices.

5 Beat butter, rind and extra sugar in small bowl with electric mixer until light and fluffy. Beat in eggs, one at a time, until combined. (Mixture will curdle, but will come together later.)

6 Transfer mixture to large bowl; using wooden spoon, stir in almond meal, flours, polenta, sour cream and juice. Carefully spread mixture into prepared pan.

7 Bake cake in moderate oven about 1¼ hours. Stand cake in pan 15 minutes before turning onto serving plate. Serve cake warm with lemon mascarpone.

LEMON MASCARPONE Combine ingredients in small bowl; whisk until smooth.

serves 12

cinnamon teacake

PREPARATION TIME 15 MINUTES
COOKING TIME 30 MINUTES

Taking care to thoroughly beat the butter, vanilla extract, sugar and egg will result in this cake having a light-as-air texture.

1 Preheat oven to moderate. Grease deep 20cm-round cake pan; line base with baking paper.

2 Beat softened butter, extract, sugar and egg in small bowl with electric mixer until very light and fluffy; this process will take between 5 and 10 minutes, depending on type of mixer used.

3 Using wooden spoon, gently stir in sifted flour and milk. Spread mixture into prepared pan.

4 Bake cake in moderate oven about 30 minutes. Stand cake 5 minutes before turning cake top-side up onto wire rack; brush top with melted butter, sprinkle with combined cinnamon and extra sugar. Serve warm with butter, if desired.

serves 10

60g butter, softened

1 teaspoon vanilla extract

⅔ cup (150g) caster sugar

1 egg

1 cup (150g) self-raising flour

⅓ cup (80ml) milk

10g butter, extra, melted

1 teaspoon ground cinnamon

1 tablespoon caster sugar, extra

TIPS To change the cake's flavour, omit the vanilla and substitute the essence of your choice, or beat in 2 teaspoons finely grated citrus rind (orange, lemon, lime or mandarin) with the butter mixture.
Melt the extra butter in microwave oven on HIGH (100%) for 10 seconds.
Cake best eaten immediately.

Aromatic cinnamon adds verve to this homely cake.

PREPARATION TIME 25 MINUTES

COOKING TIME 25 MINUTES

(PLUS COOLING TIME)

best-ever sponge cake

4 eggs

¾ cup (165g) caster sugar

1 cup (150g) self-raising flour

1 tablespoon cornflour

10g butter, softened

⅓ cup (80ml) hot water

⅓ cup (110g) lemon butter

¾ cup (180ml) thickened cream, whipped

1 tablespoon icing sugar mixture

TIPS If you don't like using your hand, use a large metal spoon or a rubber or plastic spatula to mix ingredients.
Sponge is best made on day of serving. Refrigerate sponge if it is to be filled more than an hour ahead. Unfilled sponge can be frozen for up to one month.

1 Preheat oven to moderate. Grease two deep 20cm-round cake pans.

2 Beat eggs in large bowl with electric mixer until thick and foamy. Gradually add sugar, about a tablespoon at a time, beating until sugar is dissolved between additions. Total beating time should be about 10 minutes.

3 Sift flour and cornflour together three times onto paper. Sift flour mixture over egg mixture; using one hand like a rake, quickly and lightly fold and pull flour mixture through egg mixture, using the side of your hand as a scraper to make sure all the ingredients are combined.

4 Pour combined butter and the water down side of bowl; using one hand, fold through egg mixture. Pour mixture evenly into prepared pans; using metal spatula, spread mixture to edges of pans.

5 Bake sponges in moderate oven about 25 minutes. Immediately sponges are baked, turn onto wire racks covered with baking paper; turn top-side up to cool.

6 Place one sponge on serving plate, spread with lemon butter and whipped cream. Top with remaining cake, dust with sifted icing sugar.

serves 8

Sift combined flour and cornflour over the egg mixture.

Using your hand as a rake, lightly fold flour into the egg mixture.

Use your hand as a scraper to gently combine all ingredients.

gluten-free orange syrup cake

PREPARATION TIME 25 MINUTES
COOKING TIME 1 HOUR 15 MINUTES

1 Preheat oven to moderate. Grease 21cm baba cake pan.

2 Beat butter, rind and sugar in medium bowl with electric mixer until light and fluffy. Add eggs, one at a time, beating until just combined between additions (mixture will curdle). Stir in almond meal, coconut and sifted flour and baking powder. Spread mixture into prepared pan.

3 Bake cake in moderate oven about 1 hour. Stand cake in pan 5 minutes before turning onto wire rack over oven tray.

4 Meanwhile, make orange syrup.

5 Pour hot orange syrup over hot cake; serve warm or cold.

ORANGE SYRUP Peel rind thinly from orange; cut rind into thin strips. Squeeze juice from orange (you need ⅓-cup/80ml) into small pan; stir in rind, sugar and water. Stir over heat, without boiling, until sugar dissolves. Simmer, uncovered, without stirring, 10 minutes.

serves 8

185g butter, chopped

1 tablespoon finely grated orange rind

1¼ cups (275g) caster sugar

6 eggs

3 cups (375g) almond meal

¾ cup (60g) desiccated coconut

¾ cup (110g) rice flour

1 teaspoon gluten-free baking powder

ORANGE SYRUP

1 large orange (300g)

⅓ cup (75g) caster sugar

⅓ cup (80ml) water

TIP Store the cake in refrigerator for up to two days. Cake not suitable to freeze.

Syrup cakes are popular in many parts of the world, using local spices or fruit to add moisture and flavour.

plum and hazelnut upside-down cake

PREPARATION TIME 15 MINUTES
COOKING TIME 1 HOUR

50g butter, chopped

½ cup (110g) firmly packed brown sugar

6 medium plums (680g), halved, stones removed

185g butter, softened, extra

1 cup (220g) firmly packed brown sugar, extra

3 eggs

½ cup (50g) hazelnut meal

½ cup (75g) self-raising flour

½ cup (75g) plain flour

1 Preheat oven to moderate. Grease deep 22cm-round cake pan; line base with baking paper.

2 Combine butter and sugar in small saucepan, stir over low heat until smooth; pour over cake pan base. Place plums, cut side down, over pan base.

3 Beat extra butter and extra sugar in small bowl with electric mixer until creamy. Add eggs, one at a time, beating until combined between additions; transfer mixture to large bowl.

4 Stir in hazelnut meal and sifted flours; spread mixture into prepared pan.

5 Bake cake in moderate oven about 1 hour. Stand cake in pan 5 minutes before turning onto serving plate.

TIPS Cake best made on day of serving. Not suitable to freeze.

serves 8

Turn tradition upside down with a deliciously different combination of flavours.

low-fat chocolate cake

PREPARATION TIME 15 MINUTES
COOKING TIME 50 MINUTES
(PLUS COOLING TIME)

1 Preheat oven to moderate. Spray 21cm baba cake pan with cooking-oil spray.

2 Combine jam, brown sugar, sifted cocoa, milk, coffee and butter in medium saucepan. Stir over low heat until butter is melted and mixture is smooth (do not boil). Cool.

3 Beat eggs and caster sugar in small bowl with electric mixer until thick and pale. Transfer mixture to large bowl. Stir in sifted flours and chocolate mixture. Pour mixture into prepared pan.

4 Bake cake in moderate oven about 45 minutes. Stand cake in pan 5 minutes before turning onto wire rack to cool.

5 Serve cake dusted with sifted icing, if desired.

serves 12

½ cup (160g) plum jam

½ cup (110g) firmly packed brown sugar

½ cup (50g) cocoa powder

¾ cup (180ml) skim evaporated milk

2 teaspoons dry instant coffee

50g butter

2 eggs

½ cup (110g) caster sugar

1 cup (150g) self-raising flour

⅓ cup (50g) plain flour

2 teaspoons icing sugar mixture

TIP Cake best made on day of serving. Not suitable to freeze.

Too good to be true – now we can have our cake and eat it too.

250g butter, chopped coarsely

150g dark eating chocolate, chopped coarsely

2 cups (440g) caster sugar

1 cup (250ml) hot water

⅓ cup (80ml) coffee liqueur

1 tablespoon instant coffee powder

1½ cups (225g) plain flour

¼ cup (35g) self-raising flour

¼ cup (25g) cocoa powder

2 eggs, beaten lightly

TIPS Any coffee-flavoured (Tïa Maria, Kahlua) or chocolate-flavoured (Crème de Cacao) liqueur can be used in this recipe. The melted chocolate mixture can be prepared in a large microwave-safe bowl on HIGH (100%) in the microwave oven for about 3 minutes, pausing four times to stir during cooking time.
Cake will keep for up to one week if placed in an airtight container in the refrigerator. Cake can be frozen for up to three months.

mississippi mud cake

This popular cake is a delectable alternative to fruit cake for weddings and other occasions. It is also wonderful after dinner with coffee, served warm or at room temperature with whipped cream and berries.

1 Preheat oven to moderately slow. Grease deep 20cm-round cake pan; line base and side with baking paper.

2 Combine butter, chocolate, sugar, the water, liqueur and coffee powder in medium saucepan. Using wooden spoon, stir over low heat until chocolate melts.

3 Transfer mixture to large bowl; cool 15 minutes. Whisk in combined sifted flours and cocoa, then eggs. Pour mixture into prepared pan.

4 Bake cake in moderately slow oven about 1½ hours. (Cover cake loosely with foil during baking if it starts to overbrown.) Stand cake in pan 30 minutes before turning onto wire rack; turn cake top-side up to cool. Dust with sifted cocoa, if desired.

serves 16

family chocolate cake

PREPARATION TIME 20 MINUTES
COOKING TIME 1 HOUR
(PLUS COOLING AND REFRIGERATION TIME)

1 Preheat oven to moderate. Grease deep 26.5cm x 33cm (14-cup/3.5-litre) baking dish; line base with baking paper.

2 Combine the water, sugar, butter and combined sifted cocoa and soda in medium saucepan; stir over heat, without boiling, until sugar dissolves. Bring to a boil then reduce heat; simmer, uncovered, 5 minutes. Transfer mixture to large bowl; cool to room temperature.

3 Add flour and egg to bowl; beat with electric mixer until mixture is smooth and changed to a paler colour. Pour mixture into prepared dish.

4 Bake cake in moderate oven about 50 minutes. Stand cake in pan 5 minutes before turning onto wire rack; turn cake top-side up to cool.

5 Spread cold cake with fudge frosting.

FUDGE FROSTING Combine butter, the water and caster sugar in small saucepan; stir over heat, without boiling, until sugar dissolves. Sift icing sugar and cocoa into small bowl then gradually stir in hot butter mixture. Cover; refrigerate about 20 minutes or until frosting thickens. Beat with wooden spoon until spreadable.

serves 20

2 cups (500ml) water

3 cups (660g) caster sugar

250g butter, chopped

⅓ cup (35g) cocoa powder

1 teaspoon bicarbonate of soda

3 cups (450g) self-raising flour

4 eggs, beaten lightly

FUDGE FROSTING

90g butter

⅓ cup (80ml) water

½ cup (110g) caster sugar

1½ cups (240g) icing sugar mixture

⅓ cup (35g) cocoa powder

TIPS Choose a perfectly level-bottomed baking dish; one made from cast aluminium is the best choice, but almost any type will work. If the cake appears to be cooking too quickly in the corners of the pan, reduce oven temperature to moderately slow; this will increase cooking time by up to 15 minutes. Cake will keep for up to two days in an airtight container at room temperature, or in the refrigerator for up to four days. Frosted or unfrosted, this cake can be frozen for up to three months.

dark chocolate and almond torte

PREPARATION TIME 20 MINUTES

COOKING TIME 55 MINUTES

(PLUS COOLING AND STANDING TIME)

160g dark eating chocolate, chopped coarsely

160g unsalted butter

5 eggs, separated

¾ cup (165g) caster sugar

1 cup (125g) almond meal

⅔ cup (50g) toasted flaked almonds, chopped coarsely

⅓ cup (35g) coarsely grated dark eating chocolate

1 cup (140g) vienna almonds

DARK CHOCOLATE GANACHE

125g dark eating chocolate, chopped coarsely

⅓ cup (80ml) thickened cream

TIPS Store cake in refrigerator for up to two days. Uniced cake suitable to freeze for up to three months.

1 Preheat oven to moderate. Grease deep 22cm-round cake pan; line base and side with two layers of baking paper.

2 Stir chopped chocolate and butter in small saucepan over low heat until smooth; cool to room temperature.

3 Beat egg yolks and sugar in small bowl with electric mixer until thick and creamy. Transfer to large bowl; fold in chocolate mixture, almond meal, flaked almonds and grated chocolate.

4 Beat egg whites in small bowl with electric mixer until soft peaks form; fold into chocolate mixture, in two batches. Pour mixture into prepared pan.

5 Bake cake in moderate oven about 45 minutes. Stand cake in pan 15 minutes before turning onto wire rack; turn top-side up to cool.

6 Meanwhile, make dark chocolate ganache.

7 Spread ganache over cake, decorate cake with vienna almonds; stand 30 minutes before serving.

DARK CHOCOLATE GANACHE Stir ingredients in small saucepan over low heat until smooth.

serves 14

Ganache is a French term for a mixture of melted chocolate and thick cream.

carrot cake with lemon cream cheese frosting

PREPARATION TIME 35 MINUTES
COOKING TIME 1 HOUR 15 MINUTES
(PLUS COOLING TIME)

You need approximately three large carrots (540g) for this recipe.

1 Preheat oven to moderate. Grease deep 22cm-round cake pan; line base with baking paper.

2 Beat oil, sugar and eggs in small bowl with electric mixer until thick and creamy.

3 Transfer mixture to large bowl; using wooden spoon, stir in carrot and nuts then sifted dry ingredients. Pour mixture into prepared pan.

4 Bake cake in moderate oven about 1¼ hours. (Cover cake loosely with foil during baking if it starts to overbrown.) Stand cake in pan 5 minutes before turning onto wire rack; turn cake top-side up to cool.

5 Spread cold cake with lemon cream cheese frosting.

LEMON CREAM CHEESE FROSTING Beat butter, cream cheese and rind in small bowl with electric mixer until light and fluffy; gradually beat in icing sugar.

serves 12

1 cup (250ml) vegetable oil

1⅓ cups (295g) firmly packed brown sugar

3 eggs

3 cups firmly packed, coarsely grated carrot

1 cup (120g) coarsely chopped walnuts

2½ cups (375g) self-raising flour

½ teaspoon bicarbonate of soda

2 teaspoons mixed spice

LEMON CREAM CHEESE FROSTING

30g butter, softened

80g cream cheese, softened

1 teaspoon finely grated lemon rind

1½ cups (240g) icing sugar mixture

TIPS Use a light, blended vegetable oil, such as corn, safflower or canola.
Pecans can be substituted for walnuts.
Use a commercially made cream cheese, such as full-fat Philadelphia.
Cake will keep for up to three days, refrigerated in an airtight container.
Frosted or unfrosted, the cake can be frozen for up to three months.

sticky date pudding with caramel sauce

PREPARATION TIME 20 MINUTES
COOKING TIME 55 MINUTES

1½ cups (250g) seeded dried dates

1¼ cups (310ml) boiling water

1 teaspoon bicarbonate of soda

¾ cup (165g) firmly packed brown sugar

60g butter, chopped

2 eggs

1 cup (150g) self-raising flour

CARAMEL SAUCE

1 cup (220g) firmly packed brown sugar

100g butter, chopped

300ml cream

TIPS Store pudding in the refrigerator for up to one week.
The sauce will keep, refrigerated, in a clean glass jar with a tight-fitting lid, for about two months. Sauce not suitable to freeze.

1 Preheat oven to moderate. Grease 22cm-round cake pan; line base with baking paper.

2 Combine dates, the water and soda in bowl of food processor; place lid on processor, let mixture stand 5 minutes.

3 Add sugar and butter to date mixture; process, by pulsing, about 5 seconds or until dates are roughly chopped.

4 Add eggs, then flour; process, by pulsing, about 10 seconds or until all ingredients are combined. Scrape any unmixed flour back into the mixture with a rubber spatula; pulse again to combine ingredients. Pour mixture into prepared pan.

5 Bake pudding in moderate oven about 55 minutes. Stand pudding in pan 5 minutes before turning onto serving plate. Serve hot pudding with warm caramel sauce.

CARAMEL SAUCE Combine sugar and butter in medium saucepan, stir over high heat; using wooden spoon, stir in cream. Once butter melts, bring sauce to a boil (to prevent it boiling over, either lower the heat or remove pan from heat for a moment). Stir sauce constantly until completely smooth; serve while warm.

serves 8

A restaurant-style dessert with home-made appeal.

tiramisu torte

PREPARATION TIME 30 MINUTES
COOKING TIME 25 MINUTES
(PLUS COOLING TIME)

Tiramisu literally translated means "pick-me-up", and we have little doubt that this lusciously rich, cakey version will do just that. Vienna almonds are whole almonds that have been coated in a toffee mixture.

1 Preheat oven to moderate. Grease two deep 22cm-round cake pans; line bases with baking paper.

2 Beat eggs in medium bowl with electric mixer about 10 minutes or until thick and creamy. Add caster sugar, about 1 tablespoon at a time, beating until sugar is dissolved between additions. Gently fold triple-sifted flours into egg mixture. Divide cake mixture evenly between prepared pans.

3 Bake cakes in moderate oven about 25 minutes. Turn cakes top-side up onto wire racks to cool.

4 Meanwhile, dissolve coffee powder in the water in small heatproof bowl. Stir in marsala and liqueur; cool.

5 Beat cream and icing sugar in small bowl with electric mixer until soft peaks form; transfer to large bowl. Stir in mascarpone and ½-cup of the coffee mixture.

6 Split cooled cakes in half. Centre half of one cake on serving plate; brush with a quarter of the remaining coffee mixture then spread with about 1 cup of mascarpone cream. Repeat layering until last cake half is covered with mascarpone cream. Spread remaining mascarpone cream around side of cake; press almonds into side and top of cake. Refrigerate until ready to serve.

serves 12

6 eggs

1 cup (220g) caster sugar

½ cup (75g) plain flour

½ cup (75g) self-raising flour

½ cup (75g) cornflour

¼ cup (10g) instant coffee powder

1½ cups (375ml) boiling water

¾ cup (180ml) marsala

¼ cup (60ml) coffee-flavoured liqueur

300ml thickened cream

½ cup (80g) icing sugar mixture

750g mascarpone cheese

500g vienna almonds, chopped coarsely

TIP This cake is best made a day ahead and kept, refrigerated, in an airtight container. Unfilled cake suitable to freeze for up to one month.

raspberry and almond mascarpone cake

PREPARATION TIME 45 MINUTES
COOKING TIME 2 HOURS
(PLUS STANDING AND COOLING TIME)

500g butter, softened

3 cups (660g) caster sugar

8 eggs

2 cups (300g) plain flour

1½ cups (225g) self-raising flour

1 cup (125g) almond meal

1 cup (250ml) milk

1 cup (140g) slivered almonds, toasted, chopped finely

400g fresh or frozen raspberries

400g vienna almonds

MASCARPONE CREAM

750g mascarpone

300g sour cream

1 cup (160g) icing sugar mixture

⅓ cup (80ml) Cointreau or Grand Marnier

TIPS Store unfilled cake in an airtight container for up to two days. Split and fill cake on day of serving.
Unfilled cake suitable to freeze for up to three months.

1 Preheat oven to moderately slow. Grease deep 30cm-round cake pan; line base and sides with two layers of baking paper, extending 5cm above edge of pan.

2 Beat butter and sugar in large bowl with electric mixer until light and fluffy. Add eggs one at a time, beating until just combined between additions (the mixture may appear curdled at this stage).

3 Transfer mixture to very large bowl; fold in sifted flours, almond meal and milk in three batches. Fold in chopped almonds and raspberries, then spread mixture into prepared pan.

4 Bake cake in moderately slow oven 1 hour, then reduce oven temperature to slow and bake about 1 hour. Stand cake in pan 20 minutes before turning onto wire rack to cool.

5 Using large serrated knife, split cake into three layers. Place base layer on serving plate; spread with a third of the mascarpone cream, repeat layering, ending with mascarpone cream. Decorate top of cake with vienna almonds.

MASCARPONE CREAM Beat mascarpone, sour cream and icing sugar in large bowl with electric mixer until soft peaks form; stir in liqueur.

serves 25

gluten-free carrot cake with orange frosting

PREPARATION TIME 25 MINUTES
COOKING TIME 1 HOUR (PLUS COOLING TIME)

You will need about three medium carrots (360g) for this recipe.

1 Preheat oven to moderately slow. Grease deep 20cm-round cake pan; line base and side with baking paper.

2 Sift flours, baking powder, soda and spice into large bowl; stir in sugar, carrot and nuts. Stir in combined oil, sour cream and egg until smooth. Pour mixture into prepared pan.

3 Bake in moderately slow oven about 1 hour. Stand cake in pan 5 minutes before turning onto wire rack to cool.

4 Top cake with orange frosting.

ORANGE FROSTING Beat cream cheese and rind in small bowl with electric mixer until light and fluffy. Gradually beat in sifted icing sugar until smooth.

serves 6

1 cup (125g) soy flour or besan

¾ cup (110g) 100% maize cornflour

2 teaspoons gluten-free baking powder

1 teaspoon bicarbonate of soda

2 teaspoons mixed spice

1 cup (220g) firmly packed brown sugar

1½ cups (360g) grated carrot

1 cup (120g) chopped walnuts

½ cup (125ml) extra light olive oil

½ cup (120g) sour cream

3 eggs, beaten lightly

ORANGE FROSTING

125g cream cheese, chopped

1 teaspoon finely grated orange rind

1½ cups (240g) pure icing sugar

TIPS Store cake in refrigerator for up to two days. Uniced cake suitable to freeze for up to three months.
Besan is also known as chickpea flour. Cornflour comes in two types, wheaten and corn. Make sure you use 100% corn (maize) cornflour in this recipe.

PREPARATION TIME 30 MINUTES
COOKING TIME 2 HOURS 10 MINUTES
(PLUS COOLING AND REFRIGERATION TIME)

white chocolate mud cake

250g butter, chopped coarsely

150g white eating chocolate, chopped coarsely

2 cups (440g) caster sugar

1 cup (250ml) milk

1½ cups (225g) plain flour

½ cup (75g) self-raising flour

1 teaspoon vanilla extract

2 eggs, beaten lightly

WHITE CHOCOLATE GANACHE

½ cup (125ml) cream

300g white eating chocolate, chopped coarsely

The white chocolate mud cake has rapidly ascended the ladder to the top of the special-occasion favourite-cake list.

1 Preheat oven to moderately slow. Grease deep 20cm-round cake pan; line base and side with baking paper.

2 Combine butter, chocolate, sugar and milk in medium saucepan; using wooden spoon, stir over low heat, without boiling, until smooth. Transfer mixture to large bowl; cool 15 minutes.

3 Whisk in flours then extract and egg; pour mixture into prepared pan.

4 Bake cake in moderately slow oven 1 hour. Cover pan loosely with foil; bake about 1 hour. Discard foil, stand cake in pan 5 minutes before turning onto wire rack; turn top-side up to cool.

5 Place cake on serving plate, spread all over with white chocolate ganache. Decorate with chocolate curls, if desired.

WHITE CHOCOLATE GANACHE Bring cream to a boil in small saucepan; pour over chocolate in small bowl, stir with wooden spoon until chocolate melts. Cover bowl; refrigerate, stirring occasionally, about 30 minutes or until ganache is of a spreadable consistency.

serves 12

TIPS This cake has a high fat and sugar content, and therefore it can be difficult to determine if it is cooked. The method of testing with a skewer is not accurate. Following the baking times provided is the best guide, plus the crust on the finished cake should feel quite thick and sugary. If you require a level cake, don't cool the cake top-side up. Turn it out so that the bottom becomes the top of the cooled cake, which is covered with ganache. Unfrosted cake will keep for up to one week in an airtight container at room temperature. Frosted cake will keep for up to one week in an airtight container in the refrigerator. Freeze unfrosted cake for up to three months.

glacé peach and almond cake

PREPARATION TIME 20 MINUTES
COOKING TIME 1 HOUR (PLUS COOLING TIME)

1 Preheat oven to moderate. Grease 21cm baba cake pan.

2 Beat butter, essence and sugar in medium bowl with electric mixer until light and fluffy. Beat in eggs, one at a time, beating until just combined between additions.

3 Transfer mixture to large bowl; stir in peaches, almond meal, sifted flours, milk and brandy, in two batches. Spread cake mixture into prepared pan.

4 Bake cake in moderate oven about 1 hour. Stand cake in pan 5 minutes before turning top-side up onto wire rack to cool.

serves 6

185g butter, softened

½ teaspoon almond essence

¾ cup (165g) caster sugar

3 eggs

1 cup (250g) finely chopped glacé peaches

⅓ cup (40g) almond meal

1½ cups (225g) self-raising flour

½ cup (75g) plain flour

½ cup (125ml) milk

2 tablespoons brandy

TIPS Cake can be made two days ahead; keep, covered, in an airtight container. Suitable to freeze for up to three months.

Serve a slice on a large white plate, with a scoop of ice-cream and a grilled fresh peach – sprinkle with toasted almond slivers.

PREPARATION TIME 30 MINUTES

COOKING TIME 2 HOURS 35 MINUTES

(PLUS COOLING TIME)

last-minute Christmas cake

1kg mixed dried fruit

½ cup (100g) glacé cherries, halved

250g butter, chopped

1 cup (200g) firmly packed brown sugar

1 cup (250ml) fortified dessert wine

1 cup (150g) coarsely chopped brazil nuts

1 tablespoon finely grated orange rind

1 tablespoon treacle

5 eggs, beaten lightly

1¾ cups (260g) plain flour

⅓ cup (50g) self-raising flour

½ teaspoon bicarbonate of soda

1 cup (150g) brazil nuts, extra

¼ cup (60ml) fortified dessert wine, extra

TIPS This cake can be made three months ahead; store in an airtight container in a cool place or in the refrigerator if the weather is humid. Cake is suitable to freeze for up to three months.
We used tokay dessert wine in this recipe.

1 Combine fruit, butter, sugar and wine in large saucepan; stir over low heat until butter is melted and sugar dissolved. Bring to a boil; remove from heat. Transfer to large bowl; cool.

2 Preheat oven to slow. Line base and sides of deep 23cm-square cake pan with two layers brown paper and two layers baking paper, bringing paper 5cm above sides of pan.

3 Stir nuts, rind, treacle and eggs into fruit mixture, then add sifted dry ingredients. Spread mixture into prepared pan; place extra nuts on top.

4 Bake cake in slow oven about 2½ hours or until cooked when tested. Brush top of cake with extra wine, cover hot cake tightly with foil; cool in pan.

serves 30

The words that define our lives – "last minute".

egg-free date and nut cake

PREPARATION TIME 15 MINUTES

COOKING TIME 40 MINUTES

(PLUS COOLING TIME)

1 Preheat oven to moderate. Grease deep 19cm-square cake pan; line base with baking paper.

2 Combine honey, water and butter in medium saucepan, stir over low heat until butter melts.

3 Combine sifted flour and spices, dates and nuts in medium bowl; stir in warm honey mixture. Spread cake mixture into prepared pan.

4 Bake in moderate oven about 40 minutes. Stand cake in pan 5 minutes before turning onto wire rack to cool. Glaze with a little extra honey, if desired.

serves 9

1 cup (360g) honey

1 cup (250ml) water

30g butter

2¼ cups (360g) wholemeal self-raising flour

1 teaspoon mixed spice

½ teaspoon ground ginger

1½ cups (250g) seeded chopped dates

¾ cup (90g) chopped walnuts

¼ cup (35g) chopped slivered almonds

TIPS Cake is best made on day of serving. Not suitable to freeze.

A slice of this hearty, healthy cake is a decent breakfast on the run or a reliable mid-morning pick-me-up.

PREPARATION TIME 20 MINUTES

COOKING TIME 30 MINUTES

(PLUS COOLING TIME)

gluten-free chocolate cake

1 cup (125g) soy flour

¾ cup (110g) 100% maize cornflour

1¼ teaspoons bicarbonate of soda

½ cup (50g) cocoa powder

1¼ cups (275g) caster sugar

150g butter, melted

1 tablespoon white vinegar

1 cup (250ml) evaporated milk

2 eggs

½ cup mashed banana

2 tablespoons raspberry jam

300ml thickened cream, whipped

TIPS Store unfilled cake in airtight container for up to two days. Cake not suitable to freeze.
Sandwich cake with whipped cream close to serving.

You will need one large (230g) overripe banana for this recipe. Cornflour comes in two types, wheaten and corn. Make sure you use 100% corn (maize) cornflour in this recipe.

1 Preheat oven to moderate. Grease two 22cm-round sandwich cake pans; line bases with baking paper.

2 Sift flours, soda, cocoa and sugar into large bowl; add butter, vinegar and milk. Beat with electric mixer on low speed 1 minute; add eggs, banana and jam, beat on medium speed 2 minutes. Pour cake mixture into prepared pans.

3 Bake in moderate oven about 30 minutes. Stand cakes in pans 5 minutes before turning onto wire racks to cool.

4 Sandwich cakes with whipped cream; lightly dust with extra sifted icing sugar, or extra sifted cocoa, if desired.

serves 8

Why should wheat allergies get in the way of chocoholics?

super-moist rich fruit cake

PREPARATION TIME 30 MINUTES
(PLUS STANDING TIME)
COOKING TIME 4 HOURS
(PLUS COOLING TIME)

This cake is very moist, due to the proportion of fruit to flour, which gives it a similar texture to Christmas pudding. Great as a family dessert with custard or, traditionally, for more special occasions such as 21st birthdays and weddings.

1 Combine fruit, honey and brandy in large bowl; cover; stand overnight.

2 Preheat oven to slow. Line base and sides of deep 19cm-square cake pan with three thicknesses baking paper, bringing paper 5cm above sides of pan.

3 Beat butter and sugar in small bowl with electric mixer until just combined; beat in eggs, one at a time, until just combined between additions. (Mixture may curdle at this point, but will come together later.)

4 Add butter mixture to fruit mixture with flour; mix thoroughly with one hand.

5 Drop dollops of mixture into corners of pan to hold baking paper in position; spread remaining mixture into pan.

6 Drop cake pan from a height of about 15cm onto bench to settle mixture into pan and to break any large air bubbles; level surface of cake mixture with wet metal spatula.

7 Bake cake in slow oven about 4 hours. (Cover cake loosely with foil during baking if it starts to overbrown. Give the cake quarter turns several times during baking to avoid it browning unevenly.)

8 Remove cake from oven, brush with extra brandy. Cover pan tightly with foil; cool cake in pan.

serves 36

2¼ cups (380g) raisins, chopped coarsely

3 cups (480g) sultanas

¾ cup (110g) currants

1 cup (250g) quartered red glacé cherries

1½ cups (250g) coarsely chopped seeded prunes

⅓ cup (120g) honey

½ cup (125ml) brandy

250g butter, softened

1 cup (220g) firmly packed black sugar

5 eggs

1¼ cups (185g) plain flour

2 tablespoons brandy, extra

TIPS Rum, sherry or your favourite liqueur can be substituted for the brandy.
The fruit mixture can be made up to a month before required and stored in a cool, dark place – the refrigerator is ideal.
You can use dark brown or brown sugar rather than black, if you prefer.
Because it is quite soft, this cake is best cut cold, after refrigeration.
To store cake: wrap cold cake tightly in plastic then in foil. Wrapped cake can be kept in a cool dark place for about three months; however, if the climate is humid, it is safest to keep the cake in a sealed plastic bag or tightly sealed container in the refrigerator. Cake can be frozen for up to 12 months.

PREPARATION TIME 30 MINUTES

COOKING TIME 2 HOURS 45 MINUTES
(PLUS COOLING TIME)

moist whole orange cake

2 medium oranges (480g)

⅔ cup (110g) blanched almonds, toasted

1 cup (220g) caster sugar

1 teaspoon baking powder

6 eggs

2 cups (250g) almond meal

2 tablespoons plain flour

TIPS Store cake in an airtight container for up to two days. Suitable to freeze for up to three months.

1 Place unpeeled oranges in medium saucepan; cover with cold water, bring to a boil. Boil, covered, 30 minutes; drain. Repeat process with fresh water, boil about 1 hour or until oranges are tender; cool.

2 Preheat oven to moderate. Grease deep 22cm-round cake pan; line base and side with baking paper.

3 Process toasted blanched almonds with 2 tablespoons of the sugar until finely chopped.

4 Trim ends off oranges and discard. Halve oranges; remove and discard seeds. Process oranges, including rind, with baking powder until mixture is pulpy.

5 Beat eggs and remaining sugar in medium bowl with electric mixer about 3 minutes or until fluffy and pale in colour. Fold in almond mixture, almond meal, flour and orange pulp. Pour mixture into prepared pan.

6 Bake cake in moderate oven about 1 hour or until cooked when tested. Cool in pan.

7 Turn cake onto serving plate and dust with sifted icing sugar, if desired.

serves 10

The intensity of the flavour is retained by blanching the whole fruit, peel and all.

hummingbird cake

PREPARATION TIME 35 MINUTES
COOKING TIME 40 MINUTES
(PLUS COOLING TIME)

This moist, luscious cake from the American Deep South translates as delicious in anyone's language.
You need approximately two large overripe (460g) bananas for this recipe.

1 Preheat oven to moderate. Grease deep 23cm-square cake pan; line base with baking paper.

2 Drain pineapple over medium bowl, pressing with spoon to extract as much syrup as possible. Reserve ¼ cup (60ml) syrup.

3 Sift flours, soda, spices and sugar into large bowl. Using wooden spoon, stir in drained pineapple, reserved syrup, coconut, banana, egg and oil; pour into prepared pan.

4 Bake cake in moderate oven about 40 minutes. Stand cake in pan 5 minutes before turning onto wire rack; turn cake top-side up to cool.

5 Spread cold cake with cream cheese frosting.

CREAM CHEESE FROSTING Beat butter, cream cheese and extract in small bowl with electric mixer until light and fluffy; gradually beat in icing sugar.

serves 12

450g can crushed pineapple in syrup
1 cup (150g) plain flour
½ cup (75g) self-raising flour
½ teaspoon bicarbonate of soda
½ teaspoon ground cinnamon
½ teaspoon ground ginger
1 cup (220g) firmly packed brown sugar
½ cup (45g) desiccated coconut
1 cup mashed banana
2 eggs, beaten lightly
¾ cup (180ml) vegetable oil

CREAM CHEESE FROSTING

30g butter, softened
60g cream cheese, softened
1 teaspoon vanilla extract
1½ cups (240g) icing sugar mixture

TIPS Use a light, blended vegetable oil, such as corn, safflower or canola.
Use commercially made cream cheese, such as full-fat Philadelphia.
The pineapple must be well drained; too much syrup will give you a heavy cake. Canned crushed pineapple gives better results than blended or processed fresh or canned pieces.
Cake will keep for up to three days in an airtight container in the refrigerator. Frosted or unfrosted, the cake can be frozen for up to three months.

banana cake with passionfruit icing

PREPARATION TIME 35 MINUTES

COOKING TIME 50 MINUTES

(PLUS COOLING TIME)

125g butter, softened

¾ cup (150g) firmly packed brown sugar

2 eggs

1½ cups (225g) self-raising flour

½ teaspoon bicarbonate of soda

1 teaspoon mixed spice

1 cup mashed banana

½ cup (120g) sour cream

¼ cup (60ml) milk

PASSIONFRUIT ICING

1½ cups (240g) icing sugar mixture

1 teaspoon soft butter

2 tablespoons passionfruit pulp, approximately

You need approximately two large overripe bananas (460g) for this recipe.

1 Preheat oven to moderate. Grease 15cm x 25cm loaf pan; line base with baking paper.

2 Beat butter and sugar in small bowl with electric mixer until light and fluffy. Beat in eggs, one at a time, until combined. Transfer mixture to large bowl; using wooden spoon, stir in sifted dry ingredients, banana, sour cream and milk. Spread mixture into prepared pan.

3 Bake cake in moderate oven about 50 minutes. Stand cake in pan 5 minutes before turning onto wire rack; turn cake top-side up to cool.

4 Spread cold cake with passionfruit icing.

PASSIONFRUIT ICING Place icing sugar in small heatproof bowl; stir in butter and enough pulp to give a firm paste. Stir over hot water until icing is of spreading consistency, taking care not to overheat; use immediately.

serves 10

TIPS It is important the bananas are overripe: if they are underripe, the cake will be too heavy.

The icing must be made in a heatproof bowl, preferably one made from glass or china. Stand the bowl over a saucepan of barely simmering water or in a sink filled with hot water; stir icing until it is just warmed and thin enough to pour easily. Use the icing immediately because it will set very quickly.

Cake will keep for up to three days in an airtight container. Unfrosted cake can be frozen for up to three months.

apricot loaf

PREPARATION TIME 15 MINUTES
COOKING TIME 1 HOUR 25 MINUTES
(PLUS COOLING TIME)

1 Preheat oven to slow. Grease 14cm x 21cm loaf pan; line base and sides with baking paper, bringing paper 2cm above sides of pan.

2 Place apricots, nectar and sugars in medium saucepan. Bring to a boil then simmer, covered, 5 minutes, stirring occasionally. Remove from heat; add butter, stir until melted. Transfer mixture to large bowl; cover, cool to room temperature.

3 Stir egg and sifted flours into apricot mixture and spread into prepared pan.

4 Bake cake in slow oven about 1¼ hours. Cover hot cake tightly with foil; cool in pan.

serves 8

200g dried apricots, chopped coarsely

½ cup (125ml) apricot nectar

½ cup (110g) caster sugar

½ cup (110g) firmly packed brown sugar

250g butter, chopped

3 eggs, beaten lightly

1 cup (150g) plain flour

¾ cup (110g) self-raising flour

TIPS This loaf is delicious served warm, spread with butter.
Cake can be made two days ahead, keep, covered, in airtight container. Cake suitable to freeze for up to three months.

Toast thick slices for breakfast or serve as a cake.

PREPARATION TIME 40 MINUTES

COOKING TIME 25 MINUTES

(PLUS COOLING TIME)

3 eggs

½ cup (110g) caster sugar

1 teaspoon vanilla extract

¾ cup (100g) wheaten cornflour

¾ teaspoon cream of tartar

½ teaspoon bicarbonate of soda

¼ cup (10g) flaked coconut

¼ cup (55g) caster sugar, extra

½ cup (125ml) thickened cream

1 teaspoon icing sugar

PASSIONFRUIT CURD

⅓ cup (80ml) passionfruit pulp

⅔ cup (150g) caster sugar

2 eggs, beaten lightly

125g unsalted butter, chopped

TIPS Sponge best made on day of serving. Cake not suitable to freeze. Passionfruit curd can be made three days ahead. Use any leftover curd as a topping for ice-cream, if desired..

passionfruit sponge roll

1 Preheat oven to moderate. Grease 25cm x 30cm swiss roll pan; line base with baking paper, extending paper 5cm over long sides of pan.

2 Beat eggs and sugar in small bowl with electric mixer until mixture forms thick ribbons, about 8 minutes; add extract.

3 Sift cornflour, cream of tartar and soda three times onto sheet of baking paper; lightly fold into egg mixture. Pour mixture into pan, spread into corners. Sprinkle with coconut.

4 Bake in moderate oven about 12 minutes or until top springs back when touched lightly.

5 Place damp tea towel on bench. Top with sheet of greaseproof paper; sprinkle with extra sugar. Immediately turn cake onto sugared paper; remove lining paper. Using serrated knife, cut away edges from short sides of cake.

6 Roll cake firmly from short side with paper inside; drape tea towel over roll; cool.

7 Meanwhile, make passionfruit curd.

8 Whip cream and icing sugar in small bowl with electric mixer until soft peaks form; unroll sponge, spread with half the passionfruit curd, top with cream. Roll cake again by lifting paper and using it to guide the roll into shape.

PASSIONFRUIT CURD Combine ingredients in heatproof bowl; stir over pan of simmering water about 10 minutes or until thickened slightly. Cool.

serves 6

banana bread

PREPARATION TIME 10 MINUTES

COOKING TIME 30 MINUTES

(PLUS COOLING TIME)

You will need one large overripe banana (230g) for this recipe.

1   Preheat oven to hot. Grease 14cm x 21cm loaf pan; line base with baking paper.

2   Sift flour and cinnamon into large bowl then rub in butter. Stir in sugar, egg, milk and banana. Do not overmix, the batter should be lumpy. Spoon mixture into prepared pan.

3   Bake in hot oven about 30 minutes. Stand cake in pan 5 minutes before turning onto wire rack; turn cake top-side up to cool.

4   Cut banana bread into eight slices. Toast lightly on both sides, spread with butter, if desired.

makes 8 slices

1¼ cups (185g) self-raising flour

1 teaspoon ground cinnamon

20g butter

½ cup (110g) firmly packed brown sugar

1 egg, beaten lightly

¼ cup (60ml) milk

½ cup mashed banana

TIPS Uncut banana bread will keep in an airtight container for up to two days. Banana bread is suitable to freeze. for up to three months.

Serve thick toasted slices with banana smoothies for Sunday brunch.

PREPARATION TIME 20 MINUTES

COOKING TIME 1 HOUR

(PLUS COOLING AND REFRIGERATION TIME)

chocolate butterscotch cake

¼ cup (25g) cocoa powder

250g butter, softened

1 cup (220g) firmly packed
dark brown sugar

2 eggs

1 tablespoon golden syrup

1¼ cups (185g) self-raising flour

½ cup (125ml) milk

MASCARPONE CREAM

250g mascarpone cheese

300ml thickened cream

CARAMEL ICING

60g butter

½ cup (110g) firmly packed
dark brown sugar

¼ cup (60ml) milk

1½ cups (240g) icing sugar mixture

TIPS Do not overbeat the mascarpone
cream mixture as it could curdle.
Iced cake can be made a day ahead; keep,
covered, in refrigerator. Uniced cake suitable
to freeze for up to three months.

1 Preheat oven to moderate. Grease deep 20cm-round cake pan; line
base and side with baking paper.

2 Sift cocoa into large bowl; add remaining ingredients. Beat with
electric mixer on low speed until combined. Increase speed to
medium; beat until mixture has just changed to a lighter colour. Pour
mixture into prepared pan.

3 Bake cake in moderate oven about 1 hour. Stand cake in pan 5 minutes
before turning, top-side up, onto wire rack to cool.

4 Using large serrated knife, split cold cake into three layers. Centre one
layer on serving plate; spread with a third of the mascarpone cream
and a third of the caramel icing. Repeat with second layer and half of
the remaining mascarpone cream and half of the remaining caramel
icing; top with remaining cake layer. Cover top cake layer with remaining
mascarpone cream then drizzle with remaining caramel icing. Swirl
for marbled effect; refrigerate about 30 minutes or until icing is firm.

MASCARPONE CREAM Whisk ingredients in small bowl until soft
peaks form.

CARAMEL ICING Heat butter, brown sugar and milk in small
saucepan, stirring constantly, without boiling, until sugar dissolves;
remove from heat. Add icing sugar; stir until smooth.

serves 10

mixed berry cake with vanilla bean syrup

PREPARATION TIME 20 MINUTES
COOKING TIME 50 MINUTES

Vanilla beans – the dried, thin pods of a tropical orchid grown in Tahiti, Madagascar and Central and South America – should be kept in an airtight container in a cool, dark place.

1 Preheat oven to moderate. Grease 21cm baba cake pan thoroughly.

2 Beat butter and sugar in small bowl with electric mixer until light and fluffy. Add eggs, one at a time, beating until just combined between additions. (Mixture may curdle at this stage, but will come together later.)

3 Transfer mixture to large bowl; stir in sifted flours, almond meal, sour cream, berries and cherries. Pour mixture into prepared pan.

4 Bake cake in moderate oven about 40 minutes. Stand cake in pan 5 minutes before turning onto wire rack placed over a large tray. Pour hot vanilla bean syrup over hot cake.

VANILLA BEAN SYRUP Combine the water and sugar in small saucepan. Split vanilla beans in half lengthways; scrape seeds into pan then place pods in pan. Stir over heat, without boiling, until sugar dissolves. Simmer, uncovered, without stirring, 5 minutes. Using tongs, remove pods from syrup.

serves 8

125g butter, softened

1 cup (220g) caster sugar

3 eggs

½ cup (75g) plain flour

¼ cup (35g) self-raising flour

½ cup (60g) almond meal

⅓ cup (80g) sour cream

1½ cups (225g) frozen mixed berries

½ cup (100g) drained canned seeded black cherries

VANILLA BEAN SYRUP

½ cup (125ml) water

½ cup (110g) caster sugar

2 vanilla beans

Use the leftover vanilla bean pods to flavour a pitcher of lemonade – or dry the pieces and retire them to the coffee jar.

PREPARATION TIME 20 MINUTES

COOKING TIME 45 MINUTES

(PLUS COOLING TIME)

passionfruit buttermilk cake

250g butter, softened

1 cup (220g) caster sugar

3 eggs, separated

2 cups (300g) self-raising flour

¾ cup (180ml) buttermilk

¼ cup (60ml) passionfruit pulp

PASSIONFRUIT ICING

1½ cups (240g) icing sugar mixture

¼ cup (60ml) passionfruit pulp, approximately

TIPS Cake is best made on the day of serving. Uniced cake suitable to freeze for up to three months.

1 Preheat oven to moderate. Grease and lightly flour 24cm bundt tin or 21cm baba cake pan; tap out excess flour.

2 Beat butter and sugar in small bowl with electric mixer until light and fluffy. Add egg yolks, one at a time, beating until just combined between additions.

3 Transfer mixture to large bowl; stir in half the sifted flour and half the buttermilk, then stir in remaining flour, buttermilk and passionfruit pulp.

4 Beat egg whites in small bowl with electric mixer until soft peaks form. Fold into cake mixture in two batches. Spread mixture into prepared tin.

5 Bake cake in moderate oven about 40 minutes. Stand cake in pan 5 minutes before turning onto wire rack to cool.

6 Drizzle passionfruit icing over cold cake.

PASSIONFRUIT ICING Sift icing sugar into heatproof bowl; stir in enough passionfruit pulp to form a firm paste. Stand bowl over small saucepan of simmering water, stir until icing is a pouring consistency (do not overheat).

serves 8

Buttermilk is the liquid left from cream that has been used for making butter.

date, ricotta and polenta cake

PREPARATION TIME 30 MINUTES
(PLUS STANDING TIME)
COOKING TIME 1 HOUR 55 MINUTES
(PLUS COOLING TIME)

This is the perfect cake to serve at the end of an Italian meal, or with a cup of espresso when friends drop by in the late afternoon.

1 Preheat oven to moderate. Grease deep 22cm-round cake pan; line base and side with baking paper.

2 Combine dates and liqueur in small bowl; stand 15 minutes.

3 Meanwhile, roast nuts on oven tray in moderate oven about 10 minutes; wrap warm nuts in tea-towel, rub to remove skins. Chop nuts coarsely.

4 Reduce oven temperature to moderately slow.

5 Combine flour, baking powder, polenta, sugar, ricotta, butter and the water in large bowl; beat on low speed with electric mixer until just combined. Increase speed to medium; beat until mixture changes to a lighter colour. Using wooden spoon, stir in nuts and undrained date mixture.

6 Spread half the cake mixture into prepared pan; using metal spatula, spread ricotta filling over cake mixture in pan then cover with remaining cake mixture.

7 Bake cake in moderately slow oven 45 minutes; cover tightly with foil, bake about 1 hour. Discard foil, stand cake in pan 10 minutes before turning onto wire rack; turn top-side up to cool.

RICOTTA FILLING Combine ingredients in medium bowl, stir with wooden spoon until smooth.

serves 16

1 cup (170g) finely chopped, seeded dried dates
⅓ cup (80ml) Grand Marnier
½ cup (75g) unroasted hazelnuts
2 cups (300g) self-raising flour
1 teaspoon baking powder
⅔ cup (110g) polenta
1 cup (220g) caster sugar
1¼ cups (250g) ricotta cheese
125g butter, melted
¾ cup (180ml) water

RICOTTA FILLING

1¼ cups (250g) ricotta cheese
2 tablespoons Grand Marnier
2 tablespoons icing sugar mixture
1 tablespoon finely grated orange rind

TIPS Chopped seeded prunes or raisins can be substituted for dates.
Brandy or rum can be substituted for Grand Marnier. Hazelnuts also can be replaced with any other variety of nut you like. Just be certain you select a citrus fruit that complements the flavour of the liqueur and nuts you choose. For example, Cointreau, lemon rind and walnuts marry well, as do brandy, mandarin and pecans.
Cake will keep for up to three days in an airtight container at room temperature. Not suitable to freeze.

PREPARATION TIME 25 MINUTES
(PLUS STANDING TIME)
COOKING TIME 1 HOUR

⅓ cup (50g) poppy seeds

¼ cup (60ml) milk

185g butter, softened

1 tablespoon finely grated orange rind

1 cup (220g) caster sugar

3 eggs

1½ cups (225g) self-raising flour

½ cup (75g) plain flour

½ cup (60g) almond meal

½ cup (125ml) orange juice

ORANGE SYRUP

1 cup (220g) caster sugar

⅔ cup (160ml) orange juice

⅓ cup (80ml) water

TIPS If you don't like citrus flavouring, substitute 1 teaspoon almond essence for the orange rind, and milk for the juice in the cake, and water for the juice in the orange syrup. Lemon or mandarin flavours also blend well with the taste of poppy seeds; substitute, in equal amounts, for the orange rind and juice given in the recipe.
Cake with or without syrup can be kept in an airtight container for up to two days. Cake without syrup can be frozen for up to three months.

orange poppy seed syrup cake

A popular combination of flavours makes this syrupy cake a definite favourite. If you prefer to omit the syrup completely, the cake itself is still deliciously moist.

1 Preheat oven to moderate. Grease deep 22cm-round cake pan; line base and side with baking paper.

2 Combine seeds and milk in small bowl; stand 20 minutes.

3 Meanwhile, beat butter, rind and sugar in small bowl with electric mixer until light and fluffy; beat in eggs, one at a time, until just combined between additions.

4 Transfer mixture to large bowl; using wooden spoon, stir in flours, almond meal, juice and poppy-seed mixture. Spread mixture into prepared pan.

5 Bake cake in moderate oven about 1 hour. Stand cake in pan 5 minutes before turning onto wire rack over tray; turn top-side up, pour hot syrup over hot cake. Return any syrup that drips onto tray to jug; pour over cake.

ORANGE SYRUP Using wooden spoon, stir combined ingredients in small saucepan over heat, without boiling, until sugar dissolves. Bring to a boil; reduce heat. Simmer, uncovered, without stirring, 2 minutes. Pour syrup into heatproof jug.

serves 16

festive fruit and nut cake

PREPARATION TIME 20 MINUTES
COOKING TIME 1 HOUR 45 MINUTES

This easy and quick-to-make cake is also known as a Stained Glass, American, Canadian or Jewel cake. Refrigerating it helps make cutting easy, and it can be sliced especially finely if you use a sharp serrated or electric knife.

1 Preheat oven to slow. Grease 20cm-ring pan; line base and side with baking paper, extending paper 5cm above side.

2 Combine fruit and nuts in large bowl.

3 Beat eggs and sugar in small bowl with electric mixer until thick. Add rum, butter and sifted flours; beat until just combined. Stir egg mixture into fruit mixture. Press mixture firmly into prepared pan.

4 Make fruit and nut topping. Gently press topping evenly over cake mixture; bake, covered, in slow oven 1 hour. Uncover; bake in slow oven about 45 minutes. Stand cake in pan 10 minutes.

5 Meanwhile, make toffee topping. Turn cake, top-side up, onto wire rack over oven tray; drizzle with toffee topping.

FRUIT AND NUT TOPPING Combine ingredients in medium bowl.

TOFFEE TOPPING Combine ingredients in small saucepan, stir over heat without boiling until sugar dissolves; bring to a boil. Reduce heat; simmer, uncovered, without stirring, about 10 minutes or until mixture is golden. Remove from heat; stand until bubbles subside before using.

serves 24

TIP Store cake in airtight container for up to one month. Cake not suitable to freeze.

½ cup (115g) coarsely chopped glacé pineapple

½ cup (125g) coarsely chopped glacé apricots

1½ cups (250g) seeded dried dates

½ cup (110g) red glacé cherries

½ cup (110g) green glacé cherries

1 cup (170g) brazil nuts

½ cup (75g) macadamia nuts

2 eggs

½ cup (110g) firmly packed brown sugar

1 tablespoon dark rum

100g butter, melted

⅓ cup (50g) plain flour

¼ cup (35g) self-raising flour

FRUIT AND NUT TOPPING

⅓ cup (75g) coarsely chopped glacé pineapple

¼ cup (55g) red glacé cherries, halved

¼ cup (55g) green glacé cherries, halved

¼ cup (40g) brazil nuts

¼ cup (35g) macadamia nuts

TOFFEE TOPPING

½ cup (110g) caster sugar

¼ cup (60ml) water

upside-down toffee and banana cake

PREPARATION TIME 15 MINUTES
COOKING TIME 55 MINUTES

1 cup (220g) caster sugar

1 cup (250ml) water

2 medium bananas (400g), sliced thinly

2 eggs, beaten lightly

⅔ cup (160ml) vegetable oil

¾ cup (165g) firmly packed brown sugar

1 teaspoon vanilla extract

⅔ cup (100g) plain flour

⅓ cup (50g) wholemeal self-raising flour

2 teaspoons mixed spice

1 teaspoon bicarbonate of soda

1 cup mashed banana

TIP Store cake in refrigerator for up to two days. Not suitable to freeze.

You need approximately two large overripe (460g) bananas for this recipe.

1 Preheat oven to moderate. Grease deep 22cm-round cake pan; line base with baking paper.

2 Stir caster sugar and the water in medium saucepan over heat, without boiling, until sugar dissolves; bring to a boil. Boil, uncovered, without stirring, about 10 minutes or until caramel in colour. Pour toffee into prepared pan; top with sliced banana.

3 Combine egg, oil, brown sugar and extract in medium bowl. Stir in sifted dry ingredients, then mashed banana; pour mixture into prepared pan.

4 Bake cake in moderate oven about 40 minutes. Stand cake in pan 5 minutes before turning onto wire rack covered with baking paper; turn cake top-side up. Serve cake warm or at room temperature with thick cream, if desired.

serves 8

A harmony of flavours and the heartiness of wholemeal.

Small cakes

PREPARATION TIME 15 MINUTES
COOKING TIME 25 MINUTES
(PLUS COOLING TIME)

125g butter, softened

1 teaspoon vanilla extract

⅔ cup (150g) caster sugar

3 eggs

1½ cups (225g) self-raising flour

¼ cup (60ml) milk

GLACE ICING

1½ cups (240g) icing sugar mixture

1 teaspoon butter, softened

2 tablespoons milk, approximately

food colouring, optional

TIPS Cakes are at their best made on day of serving. Unfilled and uniced cakes can be frozen for up to one month. Once filled with cream, cakes should be refrigerated if made more than an hour ahead of time.
Use two paper patty cases in each patty pan hole for added stability for butterfly cakes.

cup cakes

1 Preheat oven to moderate. Line two deep 12-hole patty pans with paper cases.

2 Combine butter, extract, sugar, eggs, flour and milk in small bowl of electric mixer; beat on low speed until ingredients are just combined. Increase speed to medium, beat about 3 minutes or until mixture is smooth and changed to a paler colour.

3 Drop slightly rounded tablespoons of mixture into paper cases. Bake in moderate oven about 20 minutes. Turn cakes onto wire racks, turn top-side up to cool.

4 Spread glacé icing over cold cup cakes.

GLACE ICING Place icing sugar in small heatproof bowl, stir in butter and enough milk to give a firm paste. Add a few drops of food colouring, if desired. Stir over a small saucepan of hot water until icing is a spreading consistency; do not overheat.

TO MAKE BUTTERFLY CAKES Using sharp pointed vegetable knife, cut circle from top of each cake; cut circle in half to make two "wings". Divide ½ cup (160g) of your favourite jam and 300ml whipped cream among cavities. Place wings in position on top of cakes; top with strawberry pieces and dust with a little sifted icing sugar, if desired.

makes 24

coffee caramel cakes

PREPARATION TIME 15 MINUTES
COOKING TIME 20 MINUTES
(PLUS COOLING TIME)

1 Preheat oven to moderate. Grease 12-hole (⅓-cup/80ml) muffin pan.

2 Beat butter and sugar in small bowl with electric mixer until light and fluffy. Add combined coffee and the water, then beat in eggs, one at a time, beating until just combined between additions. Transfer mixture to large bowl.

3 Stir in sifted flour and milk. Spoon mixture into prepared pan. Press 3 caramel halves into the centre of each cake; cover with batter.

4 Bake in moderate oven about 20 minutes. Cool in pan 5 minutes; turn cakes onto wire racks to cool..

makes 12

125g butter, softened

⅔ cup (150g) firmly packed brown sugar

2 tablespoons instant coffee powder

1 tablespoon boiling water

2 eggs

2 cups (300g) self-raising flour

½ cup (125ml) milk

18 (130g) jersey caramels, halved

TIPS Cakes best made on day of serving. Cakes suitable to freeze for up to one month.

Offering a rich, gooey surpise inside, these treats are also good served warm with a helping of fresh whipped cream.

PREPARATION TIME 20 MINUTES

COOKING TIME 50 MINUTES

(PLUS COOLING TIME)

125g butter

½ cup (100g) firmly packed brown sugar

2 eggs

1½ cups (225g) self-raising flour

½ cup (160g) fig jam

1 cup (170g) chopped raisins

½ cup (125ml) milk

TIPS There are several different sizes and types of nut roll tins available, and it is important that you do not fill them with too much mixture. As a loose guide, the tins should be filled just a little over halfway. Some nut roll tins open along the side; be certain these are closed properly before baking. Some lids have tiny holes in them to allow steam to escape; make sure these are not used on the bottom of the tins. Well-cleaned fruit juice cans may be used instead of the nut roll tins; use a double thickness of foil as a substitute for the lids. Store fruit rolls in an airtight container for up to three days. Fruit rolls can be frozen for up to three months.

fig jam and raisin rolls

1 Preheat oven to moderate. Grease two 8cm x 19cm nut roll tins, line bases with baking paper. Place tins upright on oven tray.

2 Beat butter and sugar in small bowl with electric mixer until light and fluffy. Add eggs, one at a time, beating until just combined between additions (mixture may curdle). Transfer mixture to medium bowl. Stir in flour, jam, raisins and milk, in two batches.

3 Spoon mixture into prepared tins; replace lids.

4 Bake rolls, tins standing upright, in moderate oven about 50 minutes.

5 Stand rolls 5 minutes, remove ends (top and bottom); shake tins gently to release fruit rolls onto wire rack to cool.

serves 20

banana blueberry cakes

PREPARATION TIME 20 MINUTES
COOKING TIME 30 MINUTES
(PLUS COOLING TIME)

You will need one large (230g) overripe banana for this recipe.

1 Preheat oven to moderate. Grease 12-hole (⅓-cup/80ml) muffin pan.

2 Place butter and milk in small saucepan; stir over low heat until butter melts.

3 Beat eggs in small bowl with electric mixer until thick and creamy. Gradually add sugar, beating until dissolved between additions; stir in banana. Fold in sifted flour and cooled butter mixture, in two batches. Divide mixture among muffin pan.

4 Bake in moderate oven 10 minutes. Remove pan from oven; press frozen blueberries into tops of cakes. Return to moderate oven, bake further 15 minutes. Turn cakes onto wire racks to cool.

makes 12

125g butter

½ cup (125ml) milk

2 eggs

1 cup (220g) caster sugar

½ cup mashed banana

1½ cups (225g) self-raising flour

½ cup (75g) frozen blueberries

TIPS Cakes can be stored in an airtight container for up to three days. Cakes suitable to freeze for up to one month.

Delicious to look at, beautiful to eat.

PREPARATION TIME 25 MINUTES
COOKING TIME 1 HOUR 10 MINUTES
(PLUS COOLING TIME)

orange syrup cakes

3 medium oranges (720g)

250g butter, chopped coarsely

1½ cups (330g) caster sugar

4 eggs

¾ cup (120g) semolina

¾ cup (90g) almond meal

¾ cup (110g) self-raising flour

ORANGE SYRUP

1 medium orange (240g)

½ cup (110g) caster sugar

1 cup (250ml) water

TIPS Cakes can be made four days ahead. Not suitable to freeze.

1 Preheat oven to moderately slow. Line two 12-hole (⅓-cup/80ml) muffin pans with paper cases.

2 Coarsely chop oranges, including skin; remove and discard seeds. Place oranges in medium saucepan, add enough boiling water to cover. Bring to a boil, simmer, uncovered, about 15 minutes or until tender; cool.

3 Drain oranges, then blend or process until smooth.

4 Beat butter and sugar in small bowl with electric mixer until light and fluffy. Add eggs, one at a time, beating until just combined between additions.

5 Transfer mixture to large bowl; stir in semolina, almond meal and sifted flour, then add orange puree. Spoon mixture into prepared cases.

6 Bake in moderately slow oven about 40 minutes.

7 Place hot cakes on wire rack over oven tray. Pour hot orange syrup over hot cakes. Serve warm or cold.

ORANGE SYRUP Peel rind thinly from orange, avoiding any white pith. Cut rind into thin strips. Combine sugar and the water in small saucepan, stir over low heat, without boiling, until sugar is dissolved. Bring syrup to a boil; add rind, simmer, uncovered, 5 minutes. Transfer syrup to a heatproof jug.

makes 24

apple ginger cakes with lemon icing

PREPARATION TIME 15 MINUTES
COOKING TIME 25 MINUTES
(PLUS COOLING TIME)

You will need one large apple (200g) for this recipe.

1 Preheat oven to moderate. Grease two six-hole mini fluted tube pans or texas muffin pans.

2 Beat butter and sugar in small bowl with electric mixer until light and fluffy. Add eggs, one at a time, beat until well combined between additions. Stir in syrup.

3 Transfer mixture to medium bowl; stir in sifted dry ingredients, then apple and the water.

4 Divide mixture among prepared pans, smooth tops.

5 Bake in moderate oven about 25 minutes. Stand cakes in pan 5 minutes then turn onto wire racks to cool.

6 Drizzle lemon icing over cakes.

LEMON ICING Sift icing sugar into medium heatproof bowl, stir in butter and juice to form a paste. Place bowl over small saucepan of simmering water; stir until icing is a pouring consistency.

makes 12

250g butter, softened

1½ cups (330g) firmly packed dark brown sugar

3 eggs

¼ cup (90g) golden syrup

2 cups (300g) plain flour

1½ teaspoons bicarbonate of soda

2 tablespoons ground ginger

1 tablespoon ground cinnamon

1 cup (170g) coarsely grated apple

⅔ cup (160ml) hot water

LEMON ICING

2 cups (320g) icing sugar mixture

2 teaspoons butter, softened

⅓ cup (80ml) lemon juice

TIPS Store cakes in an airtight container for up to three days.
Uniced cakes suitable to freeze for up to three months.

It's the fabulous fusion of flavours that makes these little cakes unique.

PREPARATION TIME 35 MINUTES
COOKING TIME 25 MINUTES
(PLUS COOLING TIME)

gingerbread loaves

200g butter, softened

1¼ cups (275g) caster sugar

¾ cup (270g) treacle

2 eggs

3 cups (450g) plain flour

1½ tablespoons ground ginger

3 teaspoons mixed spice

1 teaspoon bicarbonate of soda

¾ cup (180ml) milk

VANILLA ICING

3 cups (500g) icing sugar mixture

2 teaspoons butter, softened

½ teaspoon vanilla extract

⅓ cup (80ml) milk

TIPS Store cakes in airtight container
for up to four days.
Uniced cakes suitable to freeze for up
to three months.
Icing suitable to microwave.

1 Preheat oven to moderate. Grease two eight-hole (½-cup/125ml) petite loaf pans or line 22 muffin pans (⅓-cup/80ml) with paper cases.

2 Beat butter and sugar in small bowl with electric mixer until light and fluffy. Pour in treacle, beat 3 minutes. Add eggs one at a time, beating until just combined after each addition. Transfer mixture to large bowl. Stir in sifted dry ingredients, then milk. Divide mixture among prepared pans.

3 Bake in moderate oven about 25 minutes. Stand 5 minutes before turning onto wire rack to cool.

4 Spread icing over loaves; stand until set.

VANILLA ICING Sift icing sugar into heatproof bowl; stir in butter, vanilla and milk to form a smooth paste. Place bowl over simmering water; stir until icing is a spreadable consistency.

makes 16

Dark, thick, sticky treacle and ginger are old friends.

date and walnut rolls

PREPARATION TIME 15 MINUTES

COOKING TIME 50 MINUTES

(PLUS COOLING TIME)

An old-fashioned favourite, this classic nut roll, sliced and buttered, is perfect for afternoon tea. Nut roll tins are available from cookware shops and department stores.

1 Preheat oven to moderate. Grease two 8cm x 19cm nut roll tins; line bases with baking paper. Place tins upright on oven tray.

2 Combine butter and the water in medium saucepan; stir over low heat until butter melts.

3 Transfer mixture to large bowl; stir in dates and soda, then sugar, flour, nuts and egg.

4 Spoon mixture into prepared tins; replace lids.

5 Bake rolls, tins standing upright, in moderate oven about 50 minutes.

6 Stand rolls 5 minutes, remove ends (top and bottom); shake tins gently to release nut rolls onto wire rack to cool.

serves 20

60g butter

1 cup (250ml) boiling water

1 cup (180g) finely chopped seeded dried dates

½ teaspoon bicarbonate of soda

1 cup (220g) firmly packed brown sugar

2 cups (300g) self-raising flour

½ cup (60g) coarsely chopped walnuts

1 egg, beaten lightly

TIPS There are several different sizes and types of nut roll tins available, and it is important that you do not fill them with too much mixture. As a loose guide, the tins should be filled just a little over halfway. Some nut roll tins open along the side; be certain these are closed properly before baking. Some lids have tiny holes in them to allow steam to escape; make sure these are not used on the bottom of the tins. Well-cleaned fruit juice cans may be used instead of the nut roll tins; use a double thickness of foil as a substitute for the lids. Store nut rolls in an airtight container for up to three days. Nut rolls can be frozen for up to three months.

buttery apple cinnamon cakes

125g butter, softened

1 teaspoon vanilla extract

¾ cup (165g) caster sugar

2 eggs

¾ cup (110g) self-raising flour

¼ cup (35g) plain flour

⅓ cup (80ml) apple juice

1 small red apple (130g)

1½ tablespoons demerara sugar

¼ teaspoon ground cinnamon

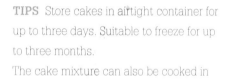

TIPS Store cakes in airtight container for up to three days. Suitable to freeze for up to three months.
The cake mixture can also be cooked in texas muffin pans.

1 Preheat oven to moderate. Grease eight-hole (½-cup/125ml) petite loaf pan.

2 Beat butter, extract and sugar in small bowl with electric mixer until light and fluffy. Add eggs, one at a time, beating until just combined between additions.

3 Fold in combined sifted flours and juice in two batches. Spread mixture into prepared pans.

4 Cut the unpeeled apple into quarters; remove core, slice thinly. Overlap apple slices on top of cakes.

5 Combine demerara sugar and cinnamon in small bowl; sprinkle half the sugar mixture over cakes.

6 Bake in moderate oven about 25 minutes. Turn cakes onto wire rack to cool. Sprinkle with remaining sugar mixture.

makes 8

A sweet crumbly topping adds a crunchy crust.

hot cross buns

PREPARATION TIME 1 HOUR
(PLUS STANDING TIME)
COOKING TIME 25 MINUTES
(PLUS COOLING TIME)

Although these delicious Easter treats are now served on Good Friday, in olden times they were thought to have holy powers and were present in many religious observances.

1 Combine yeast, sugar and milk in small bowl or jug; cover, stand in warm place about 10 minutes or until mixture is frothy.

2 Sift flour and spices into large bowl, rub in butter. Stir in yeast mixture, egg and sultanas; mix to a soft sticky dough. Cover; stand in warm place about 45 minutes or until dough has doubled in size.

3 Grease 23cm-square slab cake pan.

4 Turn dough onto floured surface, knead about 5 minutes or until smooth. Divide dough into 16 pieces, knead into balls. Place balls into prepared pan; cover, stand in warm place about 10 minutes or until buns have risen to top of pan.

5 Meanwhile, preheat oven to hot.

6 Place flour paste for crosses in piping bag fitted with small plain tube, pipe crosses on buns.

7 Bake buns in hot oven about 20 minutes or until well browned. Turn buns onto wire rack, brush tops with hot glaze; cool on wire rack.

FLOUR PASTE FOR CROSSES Combine flour and sugar in bowl. Gradually blend in enough of the water to form a smooth paste.

GLAZE Combine ingredients in small saucepan; stir over heat, without boiling, until sugar and gelatine are dissolved.

makes 16

2 x 7g sachets granulated yeast
¼ cup (55g) caster sugar
1½ cups (375ml) warm milk
4 cups (600g) plain flour
1 teaspoon mixed spice
½ teaspoon ground cinnamon
60g butter
1 egg
¾ cup (120g) sultanas

FLOUR PASTE FOR CROSSES
½ cup (75g) plain flour
2 teaspoons caster sugar
⅓ cup (80ml) water, approximately

GLAZE
1 tablespoon caster sugar
1 teaspoon gelatine
1 tablespoon water

TIPS Store buns in an airtight container for up to two days.
Uncooked buns suitable to freeze for up to three months

Combine yeast, sugar and milk; stand until mixture is frothy.

Mixture should be left in a warm place until doubled in size.

Divide dough into 16; knead into balls and place in greased pan.

Before baking, pipe crosses onto buns using a small plain tube.

All about home baking

Oven types and rack position

There are many different types of ovens and energy sources, so it is important that you get to know your oven – particularly when it comes to baking. The recipes in this book were tested in domestic-size electric ovens.

If using a fan-forced oven, check the operating instructions for best results. As a rule, reduce the baking temperature by 10°C to 20°C when using the fan during baking; cakes, biscuits and slices might also take slightly less time to bake than specified. Some ovens give better results if the fan is used for part of the baking time; it is usually best to introduce the fan about halfway through the baking time.

None of the recipes in this book have been tested in a microwave or microwave/convection oven, as the baking time and result would be different from a conventionally baked cake, biscuit or slice.

We positioned the oven racks and pan(s) so that the top of the baked cake will be roughly in the centre of the oven. If in doubt, check the manufacturer's instructions for your oven.

Several items can be baked at the same time, either on the same or different racks, provided they do not touch each other, or the oven wall or door, to allow for an even circulation of heat.

To ensure even browning, pans on different racks should exchange positions about halfway through baking time; move the lower pans to the top rack, and vice versa. This will not affect results if you do this carefully and quickly.

Best results are obtained by baking in an oven preheated to the desired temperature; this takes about 10 minutes. This rule is particularly important for cakes, biscuits or slices that bake in under 30 minutes.

Helpful hints

We do not recommend mixing cakes, biscuits or slices in blenders or processors unless specified in individual recipes.

Use an electric beater to mix cakes, and always have the ingredients at room temperature, particularly the butter. Melted or extremely soft butter will alter the texture of the baked product.

When measuring liquids, always stand the marked measuring jug on a flat surface and check at eye level for accuracy.

Spoon measurements should be levelled off with a knife or spatula. Be careful when measuring ingredients such as honey or treacle.

Faultless baking every time

Unfortunately, cakes don't always emerge from the oven looking just like our photographs. The following is a troubleshooters' guide to get you and your cakes back on track.

My butter cake wasn't perfect...

My fruit cake wasn't perfect...

Sinks in centre after removal from oven This generally means that the cake is undercooked.

Sinks in centre while still baking If the mixture is forced to rise too quickly because the oven is too hot, it will sink in the centre.

Sugary crust Butter and sugar have not been creamed sufficiently.

White specks on top Undissolved sugar, or insufficient creaming. In a light butter cake, it is better to use caster sugar, which dissolves easily.

Excessive shrinking The oven being too hot has caused cake to overcook.

Crumbles when cut Mixture may have been creamed too much, or eggs added too quickly.

Sticks to pan Too much sugar or other sweetening in recipe. If a recipe contains honey or golden syrup, or if you're using a new pan, it is wise to line the evenly greased pan with greased baking paper.

Rises and cracks in centre Cake pan too small or oven too hot. Most cakes baked in loaf, bar or ring pans crack slightly due to the confined space.

Collar around top outside edge Cake baked at too high a temperature.

Pale on top, brown underneath and sides Too large a pan, or lining paper too high around sides of pan.

Colour streaks on top Insufficient mixing of ingredients, or bowl scrapings not mixed thoroughly into cake mixture in pan.

Uneven rising Oven shelf not straight, oven not level on floor, or mixture not spread evenly in pan.

Holes in baked cake Mixture not creamed sufficiently or oven too hot.

Crusty, overbrowned, uncooked in centre Cake baked too long or at too high a temperature. Cake pan too small, causing top to overcook while cake not cooked through completely.

Fruit sinks to bottom Fruit washed, but not dried thoroughly; cake mixture too soft to support weight of the fruit (caused by over-creaming). Self-raising flour may have been used in recipe instead of plain flour. Fruit should be finely chopped so mixture can support it more easily.

Doughy in centre Cake baked in too cold an oven, or not long enough.

Burnt bottom Wrong oven position. Cake baked at too high a temperature, or incorrect lining of pans. Rich fruit cakes require protection during long, slow baking time. Cakes that are 22cm or smaller require three thicknesses of baking-paper lining; larger cakes need one or two sheets of brown paper and three sheets of baking paper.

Cracks on top Cake baked at too high a temperature.

Uneven on top Oven shelf or oven not level, or mixture not spread evenly in pan (use a wet spatula to level top of cake mixture).

My sponge cake wasn't perfect...

Creamed mixture curdles Eggs and butter not at room temperature to begin with, or eggs not added quickly enough to creamed butter and sugar mixture, or eggs used are too large for mixture to absorb the excess liquid. If eggs used are larger than 60g in weight, omit one of the number shown in ingredients list, or add only the yolk of one of the eggs. Curdled creamed mixture could cause the finished cake to crumble when cut.

Sinks in middle Self-raising flour used, or too much bicarbonate of soda. (Usually only plain flour is used in rich fruit cake, but sometimes a small portion of self-raising flour is added). Cake may not have been baked properly. To test, push sharp-pointed knife through centre to base of pan; blade surface helps distinguish between uncooked mixture or fruit and cooked mixture. Test only after minimum specified baking time.

Small white specks on top Undissolved sugar; sugar should be added gradually to beaten eggs and beaten until completely dissolved between additions.

Shrinks in oven Cake baked at too high a temperature or for too long.

Shrinks and wrinkles during cooling Insufficient baking time, or cooling the cake in a draught.

Flat and tough Incorrect folding in of flour and liquid. Triple-sifted flour should be folded into mixture in a gentle, circular motion.

Pale and sticky on top Baking at too low an oven temperature, or wrong oven position.

Crusty Baking at too high an oven temperature, wrong oven position or pan too small. Using high-sided cake pans protects the cake mixture.

Sinks in centre Pan too small, causing cake to rise quickly, then fall in the centre.

Streaks on top Scrapings from mixing bowl not mixed into sponge mixture; scrapings are always slightly darker than the full amount of mixture.

Sponge rises too quickly Oven temperature is too high.

Sponge is undercooked Oven door may have been opened during first half of baking.

getting it right

bakeware used in this book

1. 10cm-round loose-based flan tin
2. 21cm baba pan
3. deep 20cm-ring pan
4. 24cm bundt tin
5. 22cm springform tin
6. 24cm-round loose-base flan tin

bakeware used in this book

1. 8cm x 19cm nut roll tin
2. 14cm x 21cm loaf pan
3. 15cm x 25cm loaf pan
4. 19cm x 29cm rectangular slice pan
5. 20cm x 30cm lamington pan
6. 26cm x 32cm swiss roll pan
7. 8-hole (½-cup/125ml) petite loaf pan
8. 12 (⅓-cup/80ml) muffin pans
9. 6-hole mini fluted tube pan

rubbing butter into flour

Using your fingers, lightly rub cold butter into the flour, lifting it up high and letting it fall back down into the bowl. This incorporates air, which is what makes pastry light. The process should be done fairly quickly. Rub just long enough to make the mixture crumbly with just a few odd lumps here and there – it should resemble breadcrumbs.

separating egg whites

When separating egg yolk from the white, the egg has to be as fresh as possible. Crack the egg around the middle and, using both hands, break it into two halves, one in each hand. Tip the yolk back and forth from one shell to the other, letting the white trickle into a bowl while keeping the yolk in the shell. Be careful when doing this, because if one speck of yolk gets into the white, it won't be suitable for whisking.

beating egg whites with an electric mixer

When beating egg whites, what you're actually doing is incorporating air, and this increases the volume. First beat on a slow speed until everything has become bubbly, then increase the speed and continue beating until soft peaks form. Do not overbeat, as the whites will become dry and separate. The tiniest trace of egg yolk in the white means the white won't whisk; it is also important that the bowl and beaters are grease-free.

levelling off flour in a measuring cup

Lightly spoon flour into the measuring cup, adding enough flour so it forms a dome over the top of the cup. Gently shake the cup. Use the back edge of a knife to level the flour by running it along the rim of the cup to remove the excess flour. Never measure ingredients over the mixing bowl containing other ingredients as you may accidentally tip the excess into the mixture, and this could ruin the whole recipe.

making white chocolate ganache

Ganache is a French term referring to a smooth mixture of cream and chocolate, although butter may sometimes be added. Boiled cream is poured over chopped chocolate and the mixture is stirred until velvety smooth. Stand mixture until desired consistency is reached. Different flavours, such as liqueurs and extracts, also can be added.

making chocolate curls or flakes

Run a sharp vegetable peeler down the side of a large block of chocolate to create flakes. For curls, slightly soften the chocolate first, then drag a vegetable peeler down the side of the chocolate in one continuous movement. The harder you press the thicker the curls will be. Let the curls fall onto a cold baking-paper-lined tray, or a cold plate. Refrigerate until ready to use.

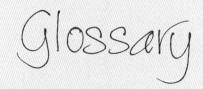

almonds

flat, pointy-ended nuts with a pitted brown shell enclosing a creamy white kernel that is covered by a brown skin.

blanched brown skins removed.

essence often interchangeable with extract; made with almond oil and alcohol or another agent.

flaked paper-thin slices.

meal also known as ground almonds; nuts are powdered to a coarse flour texture.

slivered small pieces cut lengthways.

vienna toffee-coated almonds.

aniseed

also known as anise or sweet cumin; the seeds are the fruit of an annual plant native to Greece and Egypt. Dried, they have a strong licorice flavour. Whole and ground seeds are available.

baking powder

a raising agent consisting mainly of one part bicarbonate of soda (baking soda) to two parts cream of tartar. The alkaline and acid combination, when moistened and heated, gives off carbon dioxide, which aerates and lightens the mixture during baking.

bicarbonate of soda

also known as baking soda.

bran, unprocessed

made from the outer layer of a cereal, most often the husks of wheat, rice or oats.

brazil nut

a triangular nut with a hard shell; has white flesh encased with a brown skin.

butter

use salted or unsalted (sweet) butter; 125g is equal to 1 stick butter.

buttermilk

found in the refrigerated dairy section at the supermarket. Originally just the liquid left after cream was separated from milk, today it is commercially made similarly to yogurt. Despite the implication of its name, it is low in fat.

cachous

small, round, cake-decorating sweets available in silver, gold or various colours.

cardamom

native to India and used extensively in its cuisine; can be purchased in pod, seed or ground form. Has a distinctive aromatic, sweetly rich flavour and is one of the world's most expensive spices.

chocolate

choc bits also known as chocolate chips and chocolate morsels; available in milk, white and dark chocolate. These hold their shape in baking and are ideal for decorating.

chocolate melts discs of compounded white, milk and dark chocolate; ideal for melting or moulding.

dark eating made of cocoa liquor, cocoa butter and sugar.

cinnamon

sold in stick or ground form. Dried inner bark of the shoots of the cinnamon tree.

clove

dried flower buds of a tropical tree; can be used whole or in ground form. Has a strong scent and taste so should be used minimally.

cocoa powder

also known as cocoa; dried, unsweetened, roasted then ground cocoa beans.

coconut

desiccated unsweetened, concentrated, dried, finely-shredded coconut.

flaked dried, flaked coconut flesh.

shredded thin strips of dried coconut.

corn syrup

an imported product available in some supermarkets, delicatessens and health food stores. Made from cornstarch, it is a popular ingredient in American cooking for frostings, jams and jellies.

cornflour

also known as cornstarch; used as a thickening agent in cooking.

cream

we used fresh pouring cream, also known as pure cream. It has no additives, and contains a minimum fat content of 35%.

cream, thickened a whipping cream that contains a thickener. Has a minimum fat content of 35%.

cream cheese

commonly known as Philadelphia or Philly cheese. A soft, cow-milk cheese with a fat content of at least 33%. Sold at supermarkets in bulk and packaged.

cream of tartar

the acid ingredient in baking powder; added to confectionery mixtures to help prevent sugar crystallising. Improves volume when beating egg whites, and helps to keep frostings creamy.

currants

dried, tiny, almost black raisins so-named after a grape variety that originated in Corinth, Greece.

custard

packaged pouring custard, available in cartons from supermarket dairy section.

powder instant mixture used to make pouring custard; similar to North American instant pudding mixes.

dairy-free spread

we used a polyunsaturated, cholesterol-free, reduced-fat diet spread made of vegetable oils, water and gelatine.

evaporated milk

unsweetened canned milk from which water has been extracted by evaporation.

flour

besan a flour made from ground chickpeas. Used as a thickener and as a main ingredient in Indian cooking.

gluten-free, plain available from health food stores.

plain an all-purpose flour, made from wheat.

rice a very fine flour, made from ground white rice.

self-raising plain flour sifted with baking powder in the proportion of 1 cup flour to 2 teaspoons baking powder.

soy made from ground soy beans.

wholemeal plain also known as all-purpose wholewheat flour. Plain wholemeal flour has no baking powder added.

wholemeal self-raising wholewheat flour that has baking powder added.

fruit mince

also known as mincemeat. A mixture of dried fruits such as raisins, sultanas and candied peel, nuts, spices, apple, brandy or rum. Is used as a filling for cakes, puddings and fruit mince pies.

gelatine

a colourless, almost flavourless protein used as a setting agent; should be clear when dissolved. We used powdered gelatine; it is also available in sheet form known as leaf gelatine.

ginger, ground

also known as powdered ginger. Used to flavour cakes, pies and puddings, but cannot be substituted for fresh ginger.

glacé fruit

fruit cooked in heavy sugar syrup then dried.

golden syrup
a by-product of refined sugarcane; pure maple syrup or honey can be substituted.

Grand Marnier
orange-flavoured liqueur.

hazelnut meal
also known as ground hazelnuts.

jam
also known as preserve or conserve; most often made from fruit.

jersey caramels
made from sugar, glucose, condensed milk, flour, oil and gelatine.

lemon butter
also known as lemon curd, lemon cheese or lemon spread.

macadamia nut
native to Australia. A rich, buttery nut. Store in refrigerator because of high oil content.

maple syrup
a thin syrup distilled from the sap of the maple tree. Maple-flavoured syrup or pancake syrup is not an adequate substitute for the real thing.

maple-flavoured syrup
made from sugarcane and is also known as pancake syrup. It is not a substitute for pure maple syrup.

marmalade
a preserve, usually based on citrus fruit.

marsala
a sweet fortified wine.

mascarpone cheese
a fresh, unripened, smooth, triple cream cheese with a rich, sweet, slightly acidic taste. Has a fat content of 75%.

mixed peel
candied citrus peel.

mixed spice
a blend of ground spices consisting of cinnamon, allspice, cloves and nutmeg. Used mainly in desserts and biscuits.

Nutella
chocolate hazelnut spread.

peanuts
not, in fact, a nut, but the pod of a legume.

pecans
golden-brown, buttery and rich. Good in both savoury and sweet dishes.

pepitas
dried pumpkin seeds.

pine nuts
also known as pignoli; not, in fact, a nut, but a small, cream-coloured kernel from pine cones.

pistachio
pale green, delicately flavoured nut inside hard, off-white shell. To peel, soak shelled nuts in boiling water for about 5 minutes; drain, then pat dry with absorbent paper. Rub skins with cloth to peel.

polenta
also known as cornmeal; a flour-like cereal made of dried corn (maize). Sold ground in several different textures.

poppy seeds
small, dried, bluish-grey seeds of the poppy plant. Poppy seeds have a crunchy texture and a nutty flavour. Can be purchased whole or ground in most supermarkets.

puff pastry, ready rolled
packaged sheets of frozen puff pastry, available from supermarkets.

raisins
dried sweet grapes.

ricotta cheese
a sweet, moist cheese made from cow milk, with a fat content of around 8.5%.

rolled oats
oats that have been husked, steamed-softened, flattened with rollers, dried and packaged for consumption as a cereal product.

rum, dark
we prefer to use an underproof rum (not overproof) for a more subtle flavour.

semolina
made from durum wheat milled into very fine granules; often used in Indian sweets.

sesame seeds
black and white are the most common of these tiny oval seeds.

sour cream
thick, commercially-cultured soured cream with a minimum fat content of 35%.

sugar
we used coarse, granulated table sugar, also known as crystal sugar, unless otherwise specified.

brown a very soft, fine granulated sugar retaining molasses for its characteristic colour and flavour.

caster also known as superfine or finely granulated table sugar.

black less refined than brown sugar and containing more molasses; mostly used in Christmas cakes, black sugar is available from health food stores.

coffee crystals large golden-coloured crystal sugar that enhances the flavour of coffee.

dark brown substitute with brown sugar.

demerara small-grained golden-coloured crystal sugar.

icing sugar mixture also known as confectioners' sugar or powdered sugar; pulverised granulated sugar crushed together with a small amount (about 3%) cornflour added.

raw natural brown granulated sugar.

sultanas
also known as golden raisins; dried seedless white grapes.

sunflower kernels
from dried husked sunflower seeds.

sweetened condensed milk
from which 60% of the water has been removed; the remaining milk is then sweetened with sugar.

treacle
thick, dark syrup not unlike molasses; a by-product of sugar refining.

vanilla
bean dried, long, thin pod from a tropical golden orchid grown in Central and South America and Tahiti; the tiny black seeds inside the bean are used to impart a luscious vanilla flavour in baking and desserts.

extract obtained from vanilla beans infused in water. A non-alcoholic version of essence.

extract, concentrated essence that has been reduced in a sugar syrup to a more concentrated form; stronger than essence or extract, it is an alternative to beans. Use 2:1 in place of beans or 1:2 in place of essence or extract.

walnut
a rich, buttery and flavourful nut. Should be stored in the refrigerator because of its high oil content.

yeast
a 7g sachet of dried yeast (2 teaspoons) is equal to 15g compressed yeast if substituting one for the other.

yoghurt
we used plain, unflavoured yogurt, unless otherwise specified.

Index

Facts & Figures

Wherever you live, you'll be able to use our recipes with the help of these easy-to-follow conversions. While these conversions are approximate only, the difference between an exact and the approximate conversion of various liquid and dry measures is but minimal and will not affect your cooking results.

dry measures

metric	imperial
15g	1/2oz
30g	1oz
60g	2oz
90g	3oz
125g	4oz (1/4lb)
155g	5oz
185g	6oz
220g	7oz
250g	8oz (1/2lb)
280g	9oz
315g	10oz
345g	11oz
375g	12oz (3/4lb)
410g	13oz
440g	14oz
470g	15oz
500g	16oz (1lb)
750g	24oz (11/2lb)
1kg	32oz (2lb)

liquid measures

metric	imperial
30ml	1 fluid oz
60ml	2 fluid oz
100ml	3 fluid oz
125ml	4 fluid oz
150ml	5 fluid oz (1/4 pint/1 gill)
190ml	6 fluid oz
250ml	8 fluid oz
300ml	10 fluid oz (1/2 pint)
500ml	16 fluid oz
600ml	20 fluid oz (1 pint)
1000ml (1 litre)	13/4 pints

helpful measures

metric	imperial
3mm	1/8in
6mm	1/4in
1cm	1/2in
2cm	3/4in
2.5cm	1in
5cm	2in
6cm	21/2in
8cm	3in
10cm	4in
13cm	5in
15cm	6in
18cm	7in
20cm	8in
23cm	9in
25cm	10in
28cm	11in
30cm	12in (1ft)

measuring equipment

The difference between one country's measuring cups and another's is, at most, within a 2 or 3 teaspoon variance. (For the record, one Australian metric measuring cup holds approximately 250ml.) The most accurate way of measuring dry ingredients is to weigh them.

When measuring liquids, use a clear glass or plastic jug with the metric markings. (One Australian metric tablespoon holds 20ml; one Australian metric teaspoon holds 5ml.)

Note: North America, NZ and the UK use 15ml tablespoons. All cup and spoon measurements are level.

We use large eggs having an average weight of 60g.

how to measure

When using graduated metric measuring cups, shake dry ingredients loosely into the appropriate cup. Do not tap the cup on a bench or tightly pack the ingredients unless directed to do so. Level top of measuring cups and measuring spoons with a knife. When measuring liquids, place a clear glass or plastic jug with metric markings on a flat surface to check accuracy at eye level.

oven temperatures

These oven temperatures are only a guide. Always check the manufacturer's manual.

	°C (Celsius)	°F (Fahrenheit)	Gas Mark
Very slow	120	250	1/2
Slow	140 – 150	275 – 300	1 – 2
Moderately slow	170	325	3
Moderate	180 – 190	350 – 375	4 – 5
Moderately hot	200	400	6
Hot	220 – 230	425 – 450	7 – 8
Very hot	240	475	9

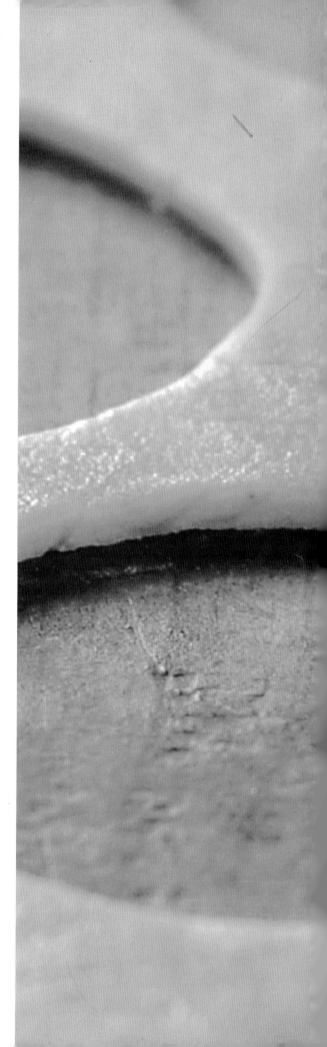

Senior Editors Wendy Bryant, Raffaela Pugliese
Designer Caryl Wiggins
Food editor Louise Patniotis
Special feature photographer Andre Martin
Special feature stylist Sarah O'Brien
Special feature food preparation Elizabeth Macri
Assistant home economist Sharon Reeve
Contributing writer Klay Lamprell
Food director Pamela Clark

ACP Books
Editorial director Susan Tomnay
Creative director Hieu Chi Nguyen
Editorial coordinator Merryn Pearse
Sales director Brian Cearnes
Publishing manager (rights & new projects) Jane Hazell
Marketing manager Katie Graham
Brand manager Renée Crea
Sales & marketing coordinator Gabriel Botto
Pre-press Harry Palmer

Production manager Carol Currie
Marketing director Nicole Pizanis
Business manager Seymour Cohen
Business analyst Martin Howes
Chief executive officer John Alexander
Group publisher Pat Ingram
Publisher Sue Wannan
Editor-in-chief Deborah Thomas

Produced by ACP books, Sydney.
Printed by SNP Leefung, China.
Published by ACP Publishing Pty Limited, 54 Park St, Sydney;
GPO Box 4088, Sydney, NSW 1028. Ph: (02) 9282 8618 Fax: (02) 9267 9438.
www.acpbooks.com.au
acpbooks@acp.com.au
To order books phone 136 116.
Send recipe enquiries to reccipeenquiries@acp.com.au

AUSTRALIA: Distributed by Network Services,GPO Box 4088, Sydney, NSW 1028.
Ph: (02) 9282 8777 Fax: (02) 9264 3278.
UNITED KINGDOM: Distributed by Australian Consolidated Press (UK),
Moulton Park Business Centre, Red House Rd, Moulton Park, Northampton, NN3 6AQ
Ph: (01604) 497 531 Fax: (01604) 497 533 acpukltd@aol.com
CANADA: Distributed by Whitecap Books Ltd, 351 Lynn Ave,
North Vancouver, BC, V7J 2C4 Ph: (604) 980 9852 Fax: (604) 980 8197
customerservioe@whitecap.ca www.whitecap.ca
NEW ZEALAND: Distributed by Netlink Distribution Company,
Level 4, 23 Hargreaves St, College Hill, Auckland 1, Ph: (9) 302 7616.
SOUTH AFRICA: Distributed by PSD Promotions (Pty) Ltd, PO Box 1175, Isando,
1600, Gauteng, Johannesburg, SA. Ph: (011) 392 6065
Fax (011) 392 6079 orders@psdprom.co.za

Clark, Pamela.
The Australian Women's Weekly Home Baked
Includes index.
ISBN 1 86396 411 8.
1. Cake. 2. Biscuits. 3. Muffins.
I. Title. II Title: Australian Women's Weekly
641.865
© ACP Publishing Pty Limited 2005
ABN 18 053 273 546

The publishers would like to thank the following for props used in photography:
Vanilla Bean, Balmain; ici et la, Surry Hills; Plenty Kitchen and Tableware, Balmain;
Orson and Blake, Woollahra; The Bay Tree, Woollahra; Imagine This, Woollahra; The
Art of Wine and Food, Woollahra; Simon Johnson, Woollahra; Myer; Wheel and
Barrow; No Chintz, Surry Hills; Tres Tabu, Northbridge; Paper Couture, Northbridge;
Tolle n Crowe, Northbridge; At The Church, Leichhardt.

Cover: Mixed berry muffins, page 12
Photographer: Brett Stevens
Stylist: Marie-Helene Clauzon
Back cover: Kisses, page 85
Photographer: Andre Martin
Stylist: Sarah O'Brien

Photographers: Alan Benson; Chris Chen; Gerry Colley; Ben Dearnley; Louise Lister;
Andre Martin; Con Poulos; Robert Reichenfeld; Brett Stevens; Ian Wallace
Stylists: Marie-Helene Clauzon; Kay Francis; Janelle Bloom; Amber Keller;
Julz Beresford; Kate Brown; Louise Pickford; Carolyn Fienberg; Sarah O'Brien